Positioning You To Meet The Mark

Prophetic Guide 100:

Your Guide For Simplistic and Resourceful Teachings

Volume 1

___

Ashley Reynolds

Prophetic Guide 100: Your Guide for Simplistic and Resourceful Teachings

By: Ashley Reynolds

Book Cover: Jasmine Miller

Published by J. Elaine Writes

www.jelainewrites.com

Printed in the United States of America

ISBN: 978-1-7332352-3-5

From the Desk of the Author:

Hello my dear young prophets. You are in a very exciting time of your life. God is awakening you to your chosen place in him as: Prophet. Congratulations on answering the call of God on your life. It has been a long, yet enjoyable years' journey writing Prophetic Guides 1&2 along with the prophetic manual. It has been my prayer and desire that you be as enlightened and educated upon the foundational principles of walking in the prophetic office or ministry. Indeed 2020 and 2021 are the years for new rising prophetic voices. It is indeed the Lord that is stirring the gifts and calling men and women all over this world to PROPHESY the word of the Lord. In Prophetic Guides 1and 2, you will find simplistic biblical principles meshed along with real life experiences. It is with hope that you find some clarity about your call to the prophetic ministry.

I was ordained in the prophetic ministry at the age of 22 years and with many years of experience and training, I felt called by the Lord to share with you what I have learned on my journey. It is with great joy that I present to you this material and pray that you get the simplistics stored up in your spirit in preparation for your next trainer to take you higher into your calling. The prophetic ministry can be weighty at times, yet God will see you through. I encourage you to pray, study Gods word, position yourself under a trusted Pastor and get you a prophetic mentor. Keep your eyes on God and flow in your calling. I encourage you to stay updated on what ashleyreynoldsministry is offering through the website below. God bless you.

Humbly Submitted,

Prophetess A. Reynolds

https://www.ashleyreynoldsministry.com/

Abstract:

Chosen

Many are called but few are chosen. The context of this Scripture can be used as a reference point for the prophetic ministry. This scripture is surrounded by the truth that while many are called to operate in the prophetic ministry, only a few have been trusted by the Lord to operate out of the prophetic office. Understand that both the prophetic ministry and the office of the prophetic has a place in the kingdom of God. However, I want you to realize that you did not choose yourself. You do not have the luxury of choosing what place you want to serve in the kingdom of God. Do not allow anyone to make you think that you can. The call to the office of the prophet comes directly from God, therefore you must not carry the mindset that you can walk in this prophetic office alone without the guidance of the Lord and a spiritual prophetic mentor. While it is possible to walk in your prophetic mantle seasonally without a mentor, there is absolutely no space for you to leave God out of this lifelong prophetic maturation process. In every season you need God! You must first realize that it is the Lord who holds the direction of your prophetic future. At times you will be sent to walk along paths that will seem too great for you to handle. You must know that He knows the way that you should take and after the Lord has tried you, you will blossom as pure gold. The goal is to get you pure. In order to embrace your prophetic journey, you must learn to trust God. Once you have learned to trust God you will then have to trust his plan for your life. This will take time, but you will come to the place that to trust God is your only option. Without trust in God

you will find it impossible to define your purpose in the prophetic arena.

Book Dedication

I dedicate Prophetic Guides 100 and 101 to Apostle Tevin Roberts and Dr. Paulette Jones Olasoji for imparting into me such wisdom as a youth growing in the prophetic office. Thank you for giving me a chance to become. I appreciate God for your providing of an Apostolic atmosphere for the provoking of change to all that came into your chambers. Thank you for living what you preached before those of us that came through your Apostolic house. I can hear in my spiritual ear what was said to Cornelius in that all of your giving and prayers have gone up before the Lord and will be answered. Know that in my life the deposits are still alive. The Lord rewards you greatly for your unselfish ways. The best is yet to come. To Pastor Selena Eason, thank you for accepting the assignment to write the forward and allowing the Holy Spirit to impart into your spirit and write through your pen spirit led words for parts 20-41. I appreciate your kindness as it is my sincere prayer that God continues to take your ministry to elevated places in Him.

To Dr. Jonathan Fowler for prophetically imparting into my soul during a transitory season of my life. The Lord continually bless you and the Improving Lives Center. To Pastor Gannt, Woman of God thank you for your sisterly friendship. Our conversations are always filled with the mysteries of heaven and great laughter. I appreciate every word that you have spoken into my life as none have fallen to the ground. I pray that as the Lord elevates you into the office of the Apostle that you will be given the revelations of the Lord to continue teaching the nation of people that the Lord has and will give you. To

Prophetess Uleasea, you have yet to tap into the greatest depth of your prophetic calling. I celebrate you and your husband as you prepare for ministry travels to prophesy a nation back to God. To Natasha Snead, we have only known one another for 2 years, yet I stand on what God said about you in that you and your daughter are called to walk in the prophetic ministry. All that you have endured in your former years shall the Lord use as a tool of opportunity to shape and mold you for His greater purpose. Always remember that there is no failure in God. Hope thou in God. Keep striving. I dedicate this piece of writing to Monique Wilson. We've only known one another for about 5 years, yet I believe in some way that it was God's design that we cross paths. Since the beginning of our connection I knew that you were a prophet of the Lord. I am proud of the growth and maturity that you have allowed the Lord to thrust you into. Wherever life leads you and your ministry, my prayer is that you remain confident in the calling whereby ye received from the Lord. Prophesy woman of God! What thou hearest in the dark, declare openly upon the housetops. Go thou in the strength of this thy might and release the word of the Lord. To Missionary (Pastor) Jasmine Miller, thank you for allowing your talents to grace the art work. You are the bomb Pastor (lol.) To Prophetess Kalima, thank you for helping to create a wonderful website which is able to professionally offer these products to those that will invest in its content. God richly bless you.

To Minister Y. Hicks, we have known one another for over 10 years and the conversations that we have had have always been meaningful and refreshing. I appreciate you for being you and for striving to live biblically in front of people and behind closed doors. There is such a ministry in you and I am excited to know you. Keep Pressing. To Pastor Chandra, the prophet who doesn't like to have prophetic conversations with me when I ask the questions. I am excited about your future and about how God will use you to bless those less fortunate and to raise the conscience of the church as it concerns business. I like to refer to you as the wealthy prophet of the Lord. Keep going sis the best is yet to come. Lastly, I dedicate this book to all of the Lord's prophets that will receive a copy of these books and manual. May you receive an impartation through the content and soar forward as the Lord permits.

I love you all,

Prophetess A. Reynolds

Forward

"For many are called, but few are chosen."- Matthew 22:14 (KJV) I have had the distinct pleasure of witnessing one of God's Chosen vessels emerge as a truly amazing Prophet of God. Prophet Ashley Reynolds has experienced the hand of God in miraculous ways. Her hunger and passion, for the Kingdom of God and the people of God, sets her apart as a cutting edge Prophet.

Prophets are distinguished by their sound and authority from Heaven. They are set aside for God's purpose within the Earth. Prophets carry a unique assignment and walk in a measure of rule and carry the weight of Glory in the Earth. Prophets are constantly under attack, making the journey lonely and long. Prophets tend to be lonely as they can't get too close to people, in order for them to hear, articulate, and navigate the Move of God, effectively. Warfare and demonic attacks are both attempts at silencing the voice of the prophet, causing the Prophetic Ministry to be long. The Prophetic Ministry is constantly engaged in battles, on behalf of God's people, seeking deliverance, miracles, signs, and wonders. Not everyone is capable of handling the responsibility and the call to the office of a Prophet. Contrary to being lonely and long, the Prophetic Ministry is also life giving. The gift of the Prophetic Ministry is speaking life, interceding, and canceling the demonic assignments and assaults against the Body of Christ.

Prophetic 100 was birth through the loins of Prophet Ashley Reynolds, serving as a point of contact to help develop, cultivate, and activate the Prophetic gift in believers. I have witnessed God take this powerful Woman of God on the journey of unlocking every spiritual gift within her, for the empowerment of the saints. Prophet Ashley Reynolds is sold out for the work of God! She has been guided by and followed the leadership of some great Apostles and Ministers of the Gospel, all of which have cultivated her in the faith. This book is life changing and written for this time. It is an instructional manual of which ministers to young and old alike, challenging everyone not to settle in a place of comfort, however to seek the Heart of God and launch out into the deep. I endorse this book and encourage every reader to prepare to be enlightened by one of God's best in the Kingdom!

Respectfully Submitted,

Apostle Tevin J. Roberts- Founder

Church of Champions

Prophetic Guide 1: Table of Contents:

Part 1: What is Prophecy?

Is prophecy for both the believer as well as for the unbeliever? What comes to mind when you hear the preacher say, "I feel like prophesying?" In this section, we will travel through the Scriptures to determine what prophecy is and what God's intent was when he ordained it to be used in the kingdom of God. We will look at how prophecy can be used as a weapon against the forces of darkness. Let's begin.

Prophecy or prediction is and has always been one of the functions of the prophet. The testimony of Jesus Christ is the spirit of prophecy. This teaches that prophecy has a spirit. There is a certain spirit that we must possess in order to tap into Christ-like prophecies. With this spirit comes a motive. The motive of the spirit of prophecy is pure. This spirit points to Christ and everything that represents him. This means that prophecy is all about exaltation. Yes, it is all about the exaltation of who Christ is. The spirit of prophecy has been given the power to locate the mind and the will of God. With this spirit of prophecy comes an assignment which is to speak forth what it knows. We can always be assured with this kind of prophecy because what it speaks forth centers around Christ. Everything in Christ manifests. So if you ever hear and receive a true word of prophecy, be excited and expect it to materialize because it's a sure word.

According to Dr. Paula Price, prophecy can be broken up and defined into two words: "pro" and "phemi." "Pro" means "beforehand or time" and "phemi" means "saying." In essence prophecy means "a saying before time." (The prophetic hand book by Dr. Paula Price) Prophecy is more forth telling than it is fore-telling. This means that it typically is more directed towards futuristic happenings than the present. Prophecy can also be defined as a "miracle of knowledge, a declaration or description or representation of something future, beyond the power of human sagacity to foresee, discern, or conjecture." (Bible study tools .com) Reading this definition clearly shows how that prophecy is not who the prophet is but it is only a function of the prophet. This means that you can be a prophet and not prophesy. I can hear in the spirit of many of you asking this question to yourself, "well, why have the title "prophet" and you are not functioning in prophecy?" Let us look at John 2:4, "4 "Woman, [a] why do you involve me?" Jesus replied. "My hour has not yet come." This verse is powerful because it reveals two things that are relevant to this section of this book. The first thing that we can see in this verse is that there was a problem and that Mary turned to the one whom she knew could fix it. Jesus, who is first, the son of God, responded to his mother's call for help with, "My time has not come." Notice that Jesus was not denying that he could not perform the miracle of wine as being the Messiah. He simply had to help Mary know that his season to perform miracles had not come.

The second powerful insight in this verse is that we can see that performing miracles was not who Jesus was, but that it was a function of his assignment in the earth as Christ. Jesus shows us that his first calling was not to produce miracles. Though Jesus would do miracles one day, his first calling was to be the Son of God. I heard the Lord say to me that we as prophets are to first discern how to be sons and daughters before we start moving in the function of our election. Many have "mastered" their gifts or functions while in the office of the prophet. However, many have not mastered how to be submitted protégés to both God and leadership. This is why many prophets find it easy to dismiss God in moments when the flesh yearns for unlawful satisfaction. This is one reason why we can dishonor our spiritual mentors with ease and have no feelings of remorse afterwards. This is why we can give a correct prophecy and go out and fornicate, lie, cheat and steal. When prophets do not learn how to be sons and daughters first, they run the danger of becoming a renegade prophet that is out of control and with whom no one can tame under Godly supervision. In John 2:4, Jesus also reveals to us how that we should be discerning of the times and the seasons we are in when it comes to functioning in our office. In John 2:4, we can see that Jesus was called and sent by God to be the Messiah with an ability to perform miracles but it was not his time. Prophets can be elected by God for the office of the prophet, and it not be their season to prophesy. True prophets are not known by their prophecies. True prophets are identified by the spirit that they carry, submission and fruit. So, just like performing miracles did not validate Jesus as being the Christ, neither does prophecy validate one as being called to the office of the prophet.

It is my belief that those whom the Lord have called to train in this season on the prophetic, will have to uproot much false information that has been embraced over the decades. Many prophets feel the need to prophesy because it makes them feel as though they are in right standing with God and in tune with the spirit. Many feel the need to "prove" their ministries to others. If budding prophets are not careful they will begin looking for validation from their peers. This happened to me at one point in my life. I too had believed that I had to have a weekly prophecy for everyone. However, My Pastor at the time comforted me by helping me to know that I did not have to pressure myself with trying to prophesy to those that were tugging on me to prophesy to them. This Pastor assured me that my greatest assignment was to worship and submit as a daughter. With doing this, I would be guaranteed to walk with integrity in my calling. I learned that I could be in tune with the spirit of God and not feel pressured to release what I heard or saw all of the time. The Lord taught me that while I was able to see or hear a thing, it did not signify that I was the chosen voice to speak it forth. However, the Lord can reveal things to the prophet so that he or she may pray and intercede on behalf of what was revealed. God reveals to redeem. I am not perfect but God is always at the fore-front of my mind. Since I have grown in my relationship with God, I now realize that what validates me the most as being a prophet of God is that I am drawn to being a daughter and reflecting both his image and character.

I boldly make the statement that, "Prophecy can deceive you." Say what Ms. Ashley! Many are deceived because they feel that because they are prophesying that they are ok with God. You can prophesy while you are in sin. Gifts and callings are irrevocable. God will not take them back. The gift will work and you will think that God is still pleased with you. Many are basing their relationship with God off of the functioning of a gift. This is dangerous. We should be measuring our relationship with God based upon our sonship with him and not by the operation of our functional gift/s. In a healthy relationship between a father and his son, it is the son's greatest desire to only do the things that would put a smile on the fathers' face. So, it is with the prophet and God relationship. The prophet should only seek to do those things that would honor God the most. The Scripture speaks on that day, how many prophesied in Jesus name but that they were still rejected. According to Jesus, this rejection was because they never "knew" or were never intimate with him. They lacked truth about who Jesus was and as a result went about in their prophetic calling failing to authentically represent him. Matthew 7:23, also shows us another reason why these prophets were denied access to enter into the kingdom of heaven. This reason was because though they were prophesying, they were also breaking the laws of God or "sinning." This is exactly what's going on in the prophetic ministries today. However, Jesus is praying for you young prophet that you will escape such a lifestyle. I am not at all promoting a lie that everyone is false in their approach to the prophetic ministry but there certainly is much sin lurking.

God does have a small remnant of prophets that are living according to the revelation which stems from their relationship with Christ the Lord.

(Matthew 7:21-23- HCSB):

"Not everyone who says to Me, 'Lord, Lord!' will enter the kingdom of heaven, but only the one who does the will of My Father in heaven. 22 On that day many will say to Me, 'Lord, Lord, didn't we prophesy in Your name, drive out demons in Your name, and do many miracles in Your name?' 23 Then I will announce to them, 'I never knew you! Depart from Me, you lawbreakers!"

I can only imagine the un-integral secretive acts that these prophesiers were doing while moving in prophecy. That word "know "can be translated as the word intimacy. Notice how those who were not intimate with God were identified as workers of iniquity and rejected. So, we can see through Scripture that it was not so much of the prophets prophesying that pleased God as much as it was the desire that God wanted them to "know" him.

Back to what prophecy is. Just as you are one vehicle away from your destination, I say that people are only one prophecy away from seeing change in their lives. There are many Scriptures that help us to best understand what prophecy is. Let us examine one of them.

2 King 20:5, " Go back and tell Hezekiah, the ruler of my people, 'This is what the Lord, the God of your father David, says: I have heard your prayer and seen your tears; I will heal you. On the third day from now you will go up to the temple of the Lord." In this Scripture is found what prophecy does in that it reveals what is hidden to the natural eyes. Prophecy is the eyes and ears of the Lord. In the old days whenever there was a prophet in the house of the Lord and he saw into the spirit, he would yell out, "I see. I see. I see." In this Scripture, we see how the Lord used the mouth of the prophet Isaiah to release the futuristic plan of the Lord concerning Hezekiah, the ruler. It is in this prophecy to Hezekiah that God brings confirmation. God wanted Hezekiah to know that what he was secretly praying to him about had reached his ears. We can also see how that not only does this prophecy bring confirmation, but it also reveals what God will do with the prayers that come before him. God said, "I will heal you." God received the prayers of Hezekiah and breathed upon them by granting him his request. The next thing that Prophecy came to do was to give the ruler Hezekiah instructions. God said, "On the third day from now you will go up to the temple of the Lord." So, we see how that prophecy has the authority from God to give instructions concerning our future life.

Let us look at another Scripture to help us see how prophecy is used. 1 Corinthians 14:3, "But when you prophesy, you will be understood, and others will be helped. They will be encouraged and made to feel better." (CEV) We can see how that prophecy carries the power to bring strength, encouragement as well as comfort. Prophecy is powerful because it carries the ability to lose those bound by spirits of heaviness, depression, sadness, hopelessness, etc. It uplifts. It brings strength. It brings a console. It is almost impossible to leave the presence of a true prophet of God feeling low in your spirit. Why? Because God has laced prophecy with the ability to oppose all oppressing spirits with the agenda to suppress the lives of people. I consider myself more of an encouraging prophet. It seems as though most that I encounter always leave the conversation with these words, "woman of God, I feel uplifted and encouraged in my spirit." Prophets that I have sat with caused me to leave the table or the conversation feeling more empowered as well. This is powerful. This means that God has given us the ability to go into people's spirits and to release anointed words that will deliver their soul out of discouragement and captivity. However, sometimes it's not that people are always low in spirit, it could very well mean that they felt as if you added a deeper depth of substance to what they already knew.

I leave this section with this scripture found in 2 Peter 1:21, "For prophecy never had its origin in the human will, but prophets, though human, spoke from God as they were carried along by the Holy Spirit." Young prophets know that true prophecy has no origin in your soul. This means that you should never get puffed up to think that prophecy began with you. All God ordained prophecies begin with God. I encourage you to stay close to God. As god uses you to prophesy, let every word from your mouth proceed with: "To God Be All Of The Glory!" Selah

Part 2: The Prophet of God

Have you ever asked yourself what a prophet is? When the Lord allows me to see and reveal that a person is a prophet their responses make me laugh. 90% of the responses are people asking that golden question: "What is a prophet?" When I ask people who they are most of them answer back with what they do. Many prophetic people get mixed up with who they are as a prophet with what they do as it relates to standing in the office. In this section, we will lay the foundation of who the prophet is and what he has been chosen to do.

What is a Prophet:

When most people hear the word prophet the first word that they think is "prophecy." I remember being a kid and growing up in a holiness and apostolic church. Whenever I knew that a prophet was coming to preach at one of our revivals, I would always get excited because I loved to see them prophesy. Their lifestyles did not matter to me as much as their prophecies. However, I was only a kid and viewed the prophetic ministry as entertainment. Most people, like myself at the time, began to think about what the prophet was coming to say more so than who they were coming to represent. This is why many were fooled. Rarely do you have people that think words such as "God, holiness or integrity etc.." when it comes to the prophet. This is one reason why the deception levels are high in the body of Christ as it relates to the prophets and prophecy. People are more concerned with hearing a "word" until they are not concerned with who these "prophets" come to represent. *Prophets are as God to the people.* The prophet is the walking future of the will of God on the earth. Prophets do not prophesy according to what is "Now." When prophets prophesy, at times they do not make sense to those that hear. This is because most prophets are before their time and when they prophesy, it is more forthtelling. It is a word that's beyond the present. They are futuristic people, which means that prophets live in the future. They are the living testament of Jesus Christ. They are chosen to stand in the light of who Jesus Christ is. Their life is a prophecy. They are mesmerized with becoming like Jesus Christ who is the chief Prophet. Though prophets are far from being perfect, it seems as though their highest aim is to reflect both the image and the character of God before man. To only have a form of godliness is unacceptable to most prophets. Most prophets understand that it does God an injustice for them to only strive to have an outer image of him while having an inner emptiness of his likeness. Most prophets realize that if they are going to benefit from the Lord while operating in their prophetic assignments that they must pursue both Gods' image and his character. Genesis 1:26: "Then God said, "Let us make humankind in our image, after our likeness, so they may rule over the fish of the sea and the birds of the air, over the cattle, and over all the earth, and over all the creatures that move on the earth." (Net Bible)

What the Prophet does:

A prophet's first function is to reflect Christ on the earth. He brings God to the People. He intercedes and then rises to convey the prophetic proverbial of God in the earth. He echo's the heart, will and mind of God. He prophesies.

What is a Prophesier:

All prophets prophesy but not all prophesiers are prophets. The simplest way to explain who prophesiers are is to liken them as unto renters. A renter is a person who pays to abide in a place only for a set time. Renters can be evicted. Renters do not own the place that they are renting. They are there only to use the property, but they do not own the property. When you rent you are only visiting. Prophesiers only visit the future but they do not live in the future as the one called to be a prophet. They are used by God to at times speak forth his mind. They do not have the liberty as the prophet to live in the mind or will of God. However, God still sees prophesiers as great use. So, let's compare the prophet from the prophesier. Simply put, the spirit of prophecy only visits the prophesier but it stays with the prophet.

Part 3: The Prophetic Rank

In this section we will examine where the prophet gets his prophetic rank from and who establishes him there. Rank from a spiritual perspective can be defined as the expanded and elevated sphere that one has been placed to prophetically operate. With prophetic rank comes an authority. Though given with the prophetic office, this authority is only activated according to the maturity level of the prophet. God knows the prophet more so than he knows himself and would not put more on him than he could bear.

What an honor and privilege for the Lord to call the prophet to service in his kingdom. The prophet of God will soar in his prophetic abilities when content within the prophetic range that the hand of God has established him or her. I would like to interject here that true growth in your prophetic comes from God and not from man. Man can give you multiple positions but it is not what you need in order to grow prophetically. As a prophet you should not be overly zealous for position. You may get it, people may glorify your name, it may cause doors to open but it may still be the thing that stifles your true prophetic maturation. True prophetic maturation is not about what happens externally as much as it is what happens internally. Let God establish you. According to Dr. Paula Price, "the expansion of a prophet's mantle determines the spherical range of his or her prophetic reach and aptitude." (The prophets handbook: a guide to prophecy and its operation pg. 209). It is the prophetic mantle that is placed upon the prophet that will reveal if he or she will operate prophetically on a local, national or international level. A part of the preparation process to get you ready to take up your prophetic mantle is warfare and battles. For each prophetic rank there are battles that you will be challenged by that will help to unlock the authority and power that you need as a prophet to operate on the level chosen for you. This is why I said that you need not depend on man giving you a position in order for you to operate, because God will give you your prophetic place in his kingdom. Please do not misunderstand me, God can use your pastor, mentor or other apostles and prophets in the church arena to help you locate your place. However, when God sends them to you to help you discern your prophetic place, it will be in direct alignment with his plan for your life. You won't be placed on a level above your rank or beneath your prophetic ability. Too many prophets are operating on levels that man assigned them and not God. We will discuss this in the section on "Displaced Prophets."

It is God which calls, chooses and controls the breadth of the prophet, not man. Tell God thank you for this truth. When God chooses you, he does so as it is in direct proportion of the inward spiritual expansion that he has provoked in your prophetic being. Let's look at a strategy that God uses to raise up the budding or young prophet, the reason he uses this strategy and how it helps the young prophet:

1. Strategy: many new prophets are restricted in their prophetic scope and range. "God purposely restricts the breadth and level of prophetic information the prophet receives or comprehends." (The prophet's Hand book: a guide to prophecy and its operation pg 209) God uses this strategy to help slow the young and zealous prophet down from moving too fast. In this moment, God is not interested in your prophetic speed as he is the prophetic integrity and accuracy that flows from both your private and public life.

2. What's God's reason for using this strategy: "It's all about your prophetic development or maturation." (The prophet's Hand Book: a guide to prophecy and its operation pg. 209) God wants you to be well equipped and prepared for the true calling of your prophetic contributions. Be it a prophetic psalmist, intercessor, preacher, or teacher etc...; God wants you well prepared.

3. How does this strategy help: "God to refine the prophet's skill, fine-tune his or her prophetic receptors, and qualify and certify the new messenger's prophetic motivations." (The prophets Handbook: a guide to prophecy and it's operation pg 209)

Let's examine some of the prophets whose prophetic rank was established by God:

1. Jeremiah- In Jeremiah 1:5;10 - The Lord and Jeremiah were in conversation when the Lord explained to him that his prophetic establishment had been ordained by him. In verse 10 is where we see the lord expressing to Jeremiah his prophetic rank and authorities.

2. Ezekiel- 3:3- 8- The Lord grants the prophet Ezekiel a prophetic rank over the house of Israel because of his assignment to them. Young prophet, know that though you are called to walk with and minister to a group of people, you must not become common with them. Many people feel as though because they walk with their leaders that they are equal in spiritual status. This can set you up to not be received when it's time for you to rise in your leadership authority to deliver a hard word to them. Save yourself the disrespect! Know who's among you. Interact with the people as led by the Lord.

3. Elisha- 1 Kings 19:16- The prophet Elisha's prophetic rank was revealed when God instructed the Prophet Elijah to give him his mantle to succeed him. This meant that the Prophet Elisha would be able to move throughout the northern kingdom of Israel as Elijah in order to exercise his prophetic rank. This prophet would have the authority to comfort kings and people of great prestige.

4. John the Baptist- This prophet was called to preach glad tidings and repentance to the gentiles. He was given the prophetic rank and authority to deal with difficult matters. He had been given rank by God and prepared by the Holy spirit in the wilderness to come out to confront people of high places as well as the common people. This was his rank.

Prophetic authorities only come from God. This is one reason why we should allow God to define our prophetic rank because it will grant us access to our true level of authority.

Waiting on God to give us our rank will also ensure our survival while in the midst of doing our prophetic assignment. Let God give you a place in HIS kingdom.

Part 4: Three Major Forms of Prophecy

Now that we have laid down the foundation of who a prophet is, let us move into the different forms of prophecy: Word of wisdom, word of knowledge, and word of prophecy. In this section we will discuss how to identify which sphere of the prophetic you operate the strongest.

⬚ Word of knowledge-. Word of knowledge is when someone gains information about someone by way of the inspiration of the Holy Spirit. It is something that you could not have known unless it was shared with you by the spirit of God. Word of knowledge predominantly deals with our "now." However, words of knowledge can also reveal information about our past. Let us examine a Scriptural example of what word of knowledge is.

⬚ In John 4: 16, Jesus said to the Samaritan woman, "go and bring our husband." The woman replied and said, "I do not have one." Jesus answered and said, "Truth" you have had five husbands and the one you are with now is not your husband."

⬚ Jesus gave the Samaritan woman a word of knowledge which dealt with both her present as well as her past. Watch the cleverness of how Jesus operates word of knowledge by using her past first. "Go and bring me your husband." The woman said, "I do not have one." Let's pause right here. In this moment the woman could have called Jesus a false prophet because he identified the man he saw in her life as her husband.

However, this was not her husband. I'm sure the woman was wondering why would a "prophet" of God tell her to bring her husband when she never had one? Jesus was leading the conversation towards confession. This is another benefit of word of knowledge in that it comes to provoke one into confessing their wrongs. Now let us continue on. After the Samaritan woman confessed that she did not have a husband, Jesus moved into her present and told her that the one with whom she was with now was not her husband. Do you see how the words of knowledge that Jesus gave this Samaritan woman went into both her past as well as her present? Do you see how the cleverness and intent of this knowledge came to bring on confession? This is the power that operates within words of knowledge.

▢ Word of wisdom- Wisdom can be linked to instructions. In it can be found the directions of what we should do after receiving a word of knowledge. Word of wisdom comes to bring comfort to our souls. It deals both with our present and our future meaning that the instructions can be something for you to do now or later. Its' ultimate agenda is to bring about change for the one that would listen to the instructions revealed. Wisdom has the power to bring healing and health to our entire being. "But the tongue of the wise brings healing." (proverbs 12:18 (b)) Let's look at a Scriptural example of the word of wisdom continuing with the story of the Samaritan woman.

⏣ After Jesus had revealed to the woman what her wrongs were and she confessed, he then moved into what she should do about it. Let's pause here. I want to point out the fact that it was not until after the woman confessed of her wrong behavior that Jesus released a word of wisdom into her life. I believe that words of wisdom do not flow until after we have had our flaws identified and agreed that they are actually our flaws. This shows a heart of submission which can now be instructed into the right direction. Now, let's examine the Words of wisdom Jesus gives this Samaritan woman. "Woman," Jesus replied, "believe me, a time is coming when you will worship the Father neither on this mountain nor in Jerusalem. You Samaritans worship what you do not know; we worship what we do know, for salvation is from the Jews. Yet a time is coming and has now come when the true worshipers will worship the Father in the Spirit and in truth, for they are the kind of worshipers the Father seeks. (John 4:21-23 (NIV)) The wisdom in these verses point to the fact of Jesus revealing to the woman on what she should do next, which was to worship. If you keep reading you will see how these words of wisdom did not only result in the conversion of this woman, but also for her whole tribe? This is the benefit of hearing and obeying a word of wisdom.

⏣ Word of prophecy- As a reminder, the word prophecy can be broken down. "Pro" means beforehand. "Phecy" means word. So, if you put both meanings together you can see that prophecy is a word spoken beforehand. Prophecy is almost always preceded with these two words: "I will or I shall." It points to what God will do. Word of prophecy deals heavily with a person's future. Prophecy unveils the mysteries of what will happen futuristically. If we look throughout the books of the prophets, we will see how they mainly spoke words of prophecy. The fates of several countries were in the mouths of these prophets. Let us examine several examples of words of prophecy through using the Scriptures:

Jeremiah 4:27

▢ "This is what the Lord says: "The whole land will be ruined, though I will not destroy it completely. Therefore, the earth will mourn and the heavens above grow dark, because I have spoken and will not relent, I have decided and will not turn back."

Isaiah 49:8-13

▢ "In the time of my favor I will answer you, and in the day of salvation I will help you ; I will keep you and will make you to be a covenant for my people, to restore the land and to reassign its desolate inheritances, to say to the captives, "come out," and to those in darkness, "Be free!" "They will feed beside the roads and find pasture on every barren hill. "They will neither hunger nor thirst, nor will the desert heat or the sun beat upon them. He who has compassion on them will guide them and lead them beside springs of water. I will turn all my mountains into roads, and my highways will be raised up. "See, they will come from afar. Some from the north, some from the west, some from the region of Siniam." " shout for joy, O heaven; rejoice, O earth; burst into song, O mountains! For the Lord comforts his people and will have compassion on his afflicted ones."

Let us sum up what we have learned so far. If you find yourself telling people about their past and present conditions and people confess their sins, then you probably operate the heaviest in word of knowledge. If you notice that you mostly give words that are instructional for people to follow so that they will see change in their current situation, then you probably operate mostly in word of wisdom. However, if you see that you are used the heaviest in words which gives hope to a person's future, then you probably operate the heaviest in word of prophecy. I want you to know that none of these are greater than the other. They all have their place in the prophetic sphere. I have seen some prophets that operate the most in only one of these forms of prophecy while seeing other prophets operate strongly in them all. It was what the Apostle Paul declared, "It is whatever the grace that is given you." After reading about the different kinds of prophecy, which one do you feel you operate the most? Hold your answer for when you get to the workbook.

Part 5: Different Types of Prophets

Would you agree that this topic of the prophet is getting more interesting as we move into different sections? Let us investigate the different types of prophets. In this section our objective is that by the end of this lesson you will be able to identify what kind of prophet you are. You will see through the Scriptures how that no one prophet is alike. You are one of a kind young prophet. Your prophetic mantle can never be compared to another. You can never be duplicated. People may try to compare you with others, but always remember that you are too unique to be compared.

We see through the Scriptures how that when one prophesies it is done to Encourage, console, and to uplift. However, because God is such a colorful God, he uses different methods of prophecy to reach his people. I heard a man of God once say that God has never left a generation without a prophet. Each generation is different. What was sufficient enough to reach the last generation may not be the method needed to effectively minister to this present generation. Let us look at the many types of prophetic methods recorded in the bible:

☐ Prophetic Intercessor- the prophet Daniel comes to mind as an example of what a prophetic intercessor looks like. Prophetic prayer goes deep into the very bowels of any situation. All prayer is spiritual in that it is spirit led. However, prophetic prayer is unique in that it has the ability to go deep into certain situations as to detect the cause of any effect. Prophetic prayer is powerful because it has the power to overturn whatever the stronghold was. "But when Daniel learned that the law had been signed, he went home and knelt down as usual in his upstairs room, with its windows open toward Jerusalem. He prayed three times a day, just as he had always done, giving thanks to his God." (Daniel 6:10- NLT)

⬚ Prophetic Psalmist- the prophetic psalmist has the innate ability to ascend into the heavenlies in order to receive melody downloads from out of the chambers of God. A great example of a prophetic psalmist would be in the life of prophetess Miriam: "Then Miriam the prophet, Aaron's sister, took a timbrel in her hand, and all the women followed her, with timbrels and dancing. Miriam sang to them: "Sing to the Lord, for he is highly exalted. Both horse and driver he has hurled into the sea." (Exodus 15:20-21- NIV)

⬚ Prophetic Poet- Jeremiah the prophet was a great poet. He was known as the weeping prophet. His writings in the book of Lamentations were poetic in its expression surrounding the sentiments of his heart and Gods' heart. (Lamentations is a prophetic poetic book which contains 5 poetic expressions.)

⬚ Prophetic Painter/ sketcher- a prophetic painter is one that captures the scenery of heaven through oil and paint. You can put them in an atmosphere of worship, and they will ascend into the heavens and receive pictures of the will of God in the "now."

King/prophet David is a great example of this with the temple sketch he received from God: 1 Chronicles 28:11-19 (GNT), "David gave Solomon the plans for all the Temple buildings, for the storerooms and all the other rooms, and for the Most Holy Place, where sins are forgiven. He also gave him the plans for all he had in mind for the courtyards and the rooms around them, and for the storerooms for the Temple equipment and the gifts dedicated to the Lord. David also gave him the plans for organizing the priests and Levites to perform their duties, to do the work of the Temple, and to take care of all the Temple utensils. He gave instructions as to how much silver and gold was to be used for making the utensils, for each lamp and lampstand, for the silver tables, and for each gold table on which were placed the loaves of bread offered to God. He also gave instructions as to how much pure gold was to be used in making forks, bowls, and jars, how much silver and gold in making dishes, and how much pure gold in making the altar on which incense was burned and in making the chariot for the winged creatures that spread their wings over the Lord's Covenant Box. King David said, "All this is contained in the plan written according to the instructions which the Lord himself gave me to carry out.""

▢ Prophetic Scribe- a prophetic scribe is one who writes for the Lord. These are the people whom the Lord releases downloads of messages through the penmanship of their hands. They are sensitive to know what the Lord is saying now or what the Lord is going to do later. I call these the "Now and Later" prophets. Many of the Lord prophets have this ability to write letters and notes to convey the heart of the father to those that would be sensitive enough to listen. It is encouraged that if you feel as though the Lord speaks with you often that you keep a notepad and pen by your side. This will ensure that you have something on hand to record the word of the Lord so that you will not forget. Moses receiving a word from the Lord is a great example of the prophetic scribe: Exodus 34:27 (NIV), "Then the LORD said to Moses, "Write down these words, for in accordance with these words I have made a covenant with you and with Israel."

⧠ Prophetic Teacher- The prophetic teacher is a very special gift to the body of Christ. It is in this sphere of the prophetic that not only are the mysteries of the Lord revealed but so are the explanations of that word. The prophetic teacher is summoned by the Lord and given a grace to travel with God through the Scriptures in an in-depth manner. These are they that labor in the scriptures to find out the history and validity of the word of the Lord. These are they that typically are called upon by pastors that prophesy a word out of their spirit and need a biblical teacher to come and explain what God was really saying to the church in that "prophetic moment." These teaching prophets are line upon line and precept upon precept. (1 Samuel 19:20 - NIV) "so he sent men to capture him. But when they saw a group of prophets prophesying, with Samuel standing there as their leader, the Spirit of God came on Saul's men, and they also prophesied." Samuel was a teacher of prophetic teachings and led a group of other prophets.

⬜ Prophetic Preacher- This kind of prophet can be defined by the life of John the Baptist. John was a preaching prophet who loved and found great pleasure with revealing the difficult things of the Lord in a very passionate way. John preached the prophetic truth so passionately until it brewed him many enemies. Typically, these kinds of prophets are not embraced by society. Most times they are fought against and shunned by their contemporaries. However, it is found that in the ministry of these types of Prophets that the Lord brings about such correction that if followed drastic change will be seen in the hearer's life.

⬜ Prophetic Cook- David the prophet said, "O taste and see that the Lord is good!" Believe it or not, but God has granted some people the wisdom on how to put certain foods together for the purposes of bringing forth healing and relief from pain. Let's read 2 Samuel 17:27-29, "Now when David had come to Mahanaim, Shobi the son of Nahash from Rabbah of the sons of Ammon, Machir the son of Ammiel from Lo-debar, and Barzillai the Gileadite from Rogelim, brought beds, basins, pottery, wheat, barley, flour, parched grain, beans, lentils, parched seeds, honey, curds, sheep, and cheese of the herd, for David and for the people who were with him, to eat; for they said, "The people are hungry and weary and thirsty in the wilderness." Shobi, Machir and Barzillai all knew what types of foods to feed David and the people because they were all weary. This food would cause the people to regain their strength.

⍰ Prophetic Minstrel- prophetic minstrels are people who have been gifted by the Lord to release heaven string instrument sounds in the earth. In these sounds alone can be found healing for the soul. They release sounds of soothe. God releases sounds that have the capacity to usher one into the presence of the Lord. In his presence is joy and pleasure forevermore. The prophet David is a great example. 1 Samuel 16:17-18, " So Saul said to his servants, "Provide for me now a man who can play well and bring him to me." Then one of the young men said, "Behold, I have seen a son of Jesse the Bethlehemite who is a skillful musician, a mighty man of valor, a warrior, one prudent in speech, and a handsome man; and the Lord is with him."

⍰ Prophetic Business- There are prophets whom the Lord will release into great wisdom and understanding about how to conduct business. They can obtain and retain quickly the strategies on how to help promote and to grow people's ideas. They are a special gift from the Lord because God has caused there to be such grace and a prophetic eye of insight on them for the purposes of helping to assist the kingdom people of the Lord into their purposes with greater ease. The tribe of Zebulun is a good example of conducting international business which involves finances. Genesis 49:13- NIV, "Zebulun will live by the seashore and become a haven for ships; his border will extend toward Sidon."

⍰ Prophetic financier- prophetic financiers are unique. They have been graced by God to develop do-able financial plans for people in need of creating financial budgets.

Normally Business and financial prophets of any church have a strong relationship and work together. The prophetic financier is one that receives insight from the Lord on the best way to finance any project that the Lord wants to do with a ministry or in a person's personal business.

- Priestly prophet- Samuel, Jeremiah and Ezekiel- all were prophets who also had a priestly anointing on their lives. The primary function of all priests was administering the church's seven sacraments: baptism, confirmation, confession, holy communion, marriage, holy orders, and anointing of the sick. Religious priests often serve as educators and missionaries. (Vault.com)

- Kingly Prophets- King David was a prophet who also had a kingly anointing on his life. The primary function of a king is to rule and delegate authority. Kings govern or oversee territories of people.

- Shepherdly Prophets- Amos- was first a shepherd and then called by God to be a prophet.

- Governmental Prophets- Joseph- was a prophet who was also chosen to interact with governmental officials and people in high places. God used him to be a prophetically and governmental voice in his era.

- Military Prophets- Deborah- was used by the Lord to lead an army into victory through her prophetic guidance, leadership and wisdom.

- Prophetic Deliverers- Moses- was called and challenged by the Lord to deliver the Israelites out of the grips of bondage while in Egypt.

- Evangelical Prophets- John the Baptist - He prophetically led soul-winning revivals that began with repentance.

- Birthing Prophets- Abraham was called by God to birth out a Jewish nation of people unto the Lord.

Young prophet I hope that after reading this section you were able to identify with what type of prophet God may desire to use you. Remember that it is possible for God to use you in more than one area. I want to encourage you to not get so caught up with 'what' type of prophet you are and to be open to however the Lord wants you to use you. Whatever the Lord wills for your life let him get all of the glory.

Part 6: The Prophet and the Scroll

In this section we will look at the importance of reading the Word of God. So exactly what do we prophesy? What does God look for when he searches for a vessel to send forth his word? You will see just how that having the Scriptures in your belly can help you become a perfected prophet as well as an accurate prophesier. You will see how valid the word of God will make you in prophesy.

Without the written word of the Lord, the prophet's prophetic gift will be limited, stifled and borderline witchery. It is the prophet's duty to develop a strong relationship with the word of God. It is the scroll that will become the reference point for the Holy Spirit to work with you. When you store up the word of God in your heart, the Holy Spirit will have identifiable substance to draw out of you when it's time for you to prophesy. The more word you store up in you will determine how deep in the spirit the Holy Spirit will take you. Many prophets are limited and operating below the level that God wants to take them in the prophetic because their scroll levels are low.

Ezekiel 2:1-2- "He said to me, "Son of man, stand up on your feet and I will speak to you." As he spoke, the Spirit came into me and raised me to my feet, and I heard him speaking to me. " The prophet had received a demand from the Lord to stand on his feet. However, it was not until the Holy spirit entered him while this word was being delivered, that the prophet was able to perform the decree of the Lord by "standing." The

30

spirit of God came in to enable the prophet to stand on the word of the Lord. Having the word of the Lord also causes your ear gate to be amplified. In John 3:12- NIV- Jesus said to his disciples, "I have spoken to you of earthly things and you do not believe; how then will you believe if I speak of heavenly things?..." It is the scroll stored in the prophet's belly, (Read Ezekiel 3:3), which will cause him to hear spiritually the mystery of heaven and to draw understanding from it. Having the scroll is like having a full well deep within.

Ezekiel 3:1 -teaches that it is after receiving the scroll that you as a prophet will be empowered to do two things: "go" and to "speak." It would be because of the word of God that the prophet would gain his strength to take a stand against hard and stiff-necked people. (Read Ezekiel 2:6-8) It was the scroll that would keep the prophet from becoming as stiff-necked as those with whom he was sent to, as well as the thing that would keep his ministry effective (Ezekiel 2:8) The writings on the scroll would be to the degree of the word that God was calling the prophet to prophesy. You can identify the kind of prophetic ministry God will use you in by the letters written on the scroll. (Ezekiel 3:5-6) What God feeds you from the scroll will develop the intellect of the people you are sent to share it with.

Ezra was a man of the scroll. The bible says that he gave himself over to the study of the law. This was because he was called to be a priest and to teach others what the spirit of the law was. Ezra had 13 others with whom 7 would sit on his right and 6 on his left for the purpose of judging the word that he preached. This should be what the prophet does by having others around them that would judge the words that they speak as it should always be in direct correspondence with the word of the Lord. The prophet should be like the priest Ezra in that he should sacrifice his life over the study of the scroll in order that he might speak forth a biblically sound word. The prophet should also study the scroll as a means of foundation for the prophetic assignments ahead of him.

What do we prophesy?

When we talk about prophesying, we are simply talking about words that flow from out of the established well of our spirits. This inner well is filled by either the logos or the rhema word; we will discuss these later. In Luke 4:17-21, Jesus spoke forth a prophetic word by using a scroll. Look at these verses: "and the scroll of the prophet Isaiah was handed to him. Unrolling it, he found the place where it is written: "The Spirit of the Lord is on me, because he has anointed me to proclaim good news to the poor. He has sent me to proclaim freedom for the prisoners and recovery of sight for the blind, to set the oppressed free, to proclaim the year of the Lord's favor." Then he rolled up the scroll, gave it back to the attendant and sat down. The eyes of everyone in the synagogue were fastened on him. He began by saying to them, "Today this scripture is fulfilled in your hearing." In these moments, Jesus had become a prime example on how that true prophecy is confirmed by the prophetic sayings of the prophets that were written on the scrolls. The safety of this scroll that Jesus used was that it was Holy Ghost inspired, meaning that it was filled with truth. When we use the word, "prophecy", what we are saying is that a person is speaking forth words that come from God in heaven. I would like to express that there will be seasons where you only prophesy the scriptures. This form of prophecy in my opinion is the safest source of prophecy because it was written by Holy inspired men. The Holy Spirit only speaks what God speaks which means that everything he does carries truth. There will be other seasons where you will speak forth Holy Spirit inspired words of knowledge. There will be seasons where there is a mixture of scripture and word of knowledge as well as seasons where you will not use words but rather your presence alone will be a prophecy. We call this prophetic acts where your words won't flow but more so your actions will prophetically speak the loudest. This has to do a lot with prophetic imagery.

Prophesy the Scripture

It is imperative that the prophet have the word stored up in their spirit. I have come to learn that God will have you to study passages of scripture now, because there is a prophecy that he will form in your spirit to tell in later times. Daniel 12:4- "But thou, O Daniel, shut up the words, and seal the book, even to the time appointed: many shall pass over, and knowledge shall be manifold." We can see through this scripture how though the prophet Daniel had received words from the Lord, he was instructed to not say anything. We see the reason as to why he was told to not say anything which was because many had not been taught and knowledge had not increased at that time. You see God has a prophetic voice for every nation and generation. It is to my understanding through this scripture that God will begin talking to and preparing prophets before time to prophesy what the word of the Lord is 2, 5,10 or maybe even 20 years into the future. Having the Scripture in your spirit gives the Holy Spirit a greater opportunity to take you deeper into the revelation of what God is saying about any matter.

Prophesy words of knowledge

This seems to be the area of prophecy that is fought the most. When you are being used to give words of knowledge it means that God is giving you information about a person or a thing that no one in the flesh could have disclosed with you. When we see prophets that call out peoples addresses, phone numbers, names, etc... people become disheartened and stand in disbelief, because they feel as if this prophet is a trickster or operating in witchcraft. Though this is true for some; it is not true for all. When you have the Holy Spirit, you have an advantage. Let's look at a certain Scripture found in 1 Corinthians 2:10- "But it was to us that God revealed these things by his Spirit. For his Spirit searches out everything and shows us God's deep secrets." When you are a prophet and you have the Holy Spirit, it will become easy for you to know secretive things that only God knows. You may say, "well, why is it important for a prophet to call out people's personal things?" That's a good question. Let's look at a scripture found in the prophetic book of Isaiah 43:1, "Now, this is what the LORD says, the one who created you, O Jacob, and formed you, O Israel: "Don't be afraid, for I will protect you. I call you by name, you are mine." It is to my understanding through the reading of this scripture that this happens because God wants to grab the attention of the one that he wants to talk to. This also reveals to the person that God is still using prophets in this day and time. Another understanding that I have through this scripture is that God wants you to know that he knows you and where you currently stand in life. He also uses words of knowledge to remind you that you are his property (rather a heathen or a saint) at that time. God cares for you.

Scripture and word of knowledge

This is the season where God will give you words of knowledge and scripture to speak. An example of this looks like this:

▢ Prophet: "I hear the name Sara Wilcox. I hear 04/23/1990."

▢ Sara Wilcox: "That's me, that's me." "That's my birthday, too." (praising God)

▢ Prophet: "Well glory to God." Sara, I hear the Lord say that your college debt is being erased. I see the numbers 45631.34."

▢ Sara Wilcox: "Glory to God. That's how much debt I owe down to the penny." (crying)

▢ Prophet: Sara, I hear this Scripture in my spirit, Deuteronomy 15:1, "At the end of every seven years you shall grant a remission of debts."

▢ Sara Wilcox: "Oh my goodness. In a week will mark the seventh year that I would have been out of school." "Glory to God."

▢ Prophet: "The Lord said that by the seventh year all of your $45631.34 debt will be erased."

Do you see how this prophet went forth in the prophetic using both words of knowledge along with the scripture? Please do not misunderstand me. The only parts of the prophetic that need scripture with it is prophecy and word of wisdom. Word of knowledge is just that. You are telling someone something about themselves that is true. The same with words of wisdom. However, with the word of wisdom there will be situations that will fit in scripture and others will not, but it will still all be from God. Let's look at some examples with words of wisdom with scripture and words of wisdom without scripture:

- A pastor looks at a member and says, "Brother Hazel, the Lord says that you need to walk 30 minutes for the next 15 days to help lower your cholesterol." This is indeed a word from the Lord because brother Hazel admits that at his last doctors visit, the doctor told him that he had high levels of cholesterol and that brisk walking would help that condition.

- Ok, now let's examine how a word of wisdom with needed scripture is released. The prophet says to sister Tangent, "Sister Tangent, the Lord said for you to go down to Havertys furniture and to take a line of credit for up to $10,000." Well sister Tangent gets a little concerned because she already owes Ashley's furniture from the last credit card and her credit score is only at 436. The prophet gives Sister Tangent this scripture found in 2 Kings 4:2, "Elisha said, "Go around and ask all your neighbors for empty jars. Don't ask for just a few." The Prophet then explains to her that if she follows the instructions she will be blessed in the end. lol

Prophetic Presence

This is the season when you do not use words but rather that you show up as the manifested word of the Lord. Prophets are typically one step ahead of the church. This means that if you are ever in doubt of what the Lord is doing in a particular season, you should look on the prophets. I know this section was long, but it was necessary.

Part 7: The Prophet and Prayer

Should the Prophet pray? If you answered yes, then you have the spirit of the Lord in you young prophet. You cannot prophesy without communicating with God, or can you? In this section you will see the importance of developing a strong prayer life with the God of all true and accurate prophecies.

1 Thessalonians 5:17 states how that we should pray without ceasing. In Luke 18:1, "Then Jesus told his disciples a parable to show them that they should always pray and not give up." "Praying always with all prayer and supplication in the Spirit and watching thereunto with all perseverance and supplication for all saints." Ephesians 6:18

There are many Scriptures that challenge the saints to pray. It is my belief that all men must pray. Prayer is the gateway into the thoughts of God. Prophets must especially pray. As we have identified what a prophet is in our earlier sections, we have determined that a prophet is a person that brings forth the message of the Lord. We also learned that there are no two prophets alike, therefore how the words of God are brought forth through his prophets varies. However, how then can a prophet of God bring forth the true word of the Lord if they are not in constant communion with the Lord? Any prophet that does not pray but always has a word to share needs to be examined through a spiritual lens. Someone should ask this prophet where they are receiving this information from. To whom have they submitted their gift in the spirit? Simply put they should be asked whom they are communicating with.

Gifts and callings are irrevocable. This means that this gift of prophecy will not be taken away on the basis if the person with the gift decides to serve the Lord or not. With the Lord, your gift is clean, pure and accurate. Your word will be laced with enough power to penetrate through the barriers which stand tall in order to block the manifestation and effectiveness of the word spoken. With your word you will have God and all of heaven backing you up. Young Prophet I encourage you to pray. Keep an open line of communication with the Lord. Always ask the Holy Spirit and your mentor/Pastor to help you carefully understand what is revealed to you.

Part 8: Familiar Spirits

Why the Prophets should stay away from this

Familiar spirits are spirits that mimic the authentic gift of prophecy. In this section you will see how though familiar spirits are unclean spirits how they can still release accurate words. How can this be? Where does this spirit come from? How can I identify it? How do I keep my vessel clear of this spirit? You will see how these familiar spirits operate and what their agenda is.

What is a familiar spirit-

A familiar spirit is a messenger of the demonic world. It has only the capacity to carry information in its mouth and not revelation. The realm of heavenly revelation is closed off to this demonic entity. It is a spirit that mimics the ministry of the prophet. It mimics the ministry of the prophet by accessing information from the spiritual world. This familiar spirit can access information by two ways:

☐ hanging around prophetic atmospheres in order that it might hear God's secrets

☐ through what has already been revealed in the past

It can gain information but not prophetic insight of the thing that it is seeking information about. Notice how that though Saul was able to communicate with a familiar spirit to gain information, it was not new information that he gained. It was information that was already told to him by the prophet Samuel when he was alive. (Read 1 Samuel 15:26-29) This shows that familiar spirits cannot go into the future to access the revelation that is stored in the spirit of God. Fresh revelation is on reserve and is only revealed to the intercessors, righteous walkers and the prophets of the Lord. The familiar spirit is a false spirit that appears as truth. Young prophets do not entertain this spirit. It is deceptive because it is limited. It is because of limitation that it must appear as if it walks in the total truth of the Lord. It is through this form of godliness and outward presentation of information that many are snatched into great deception. However, it will take having eyes of the spirit to look within the spirit of this demonic force to see that it lacks the potent prophetic revelations of the Lord. Read 1 Samuel 28:15-19- particularly verse 17....

Where does this spirit come from?

This spirit originates from the world of the demonic. This spirit comes to mimic the prophets and to deceive the believer through the operation of a gift. Read Exodus 5-8

How can an unclean spirit of familiarity be so accurate?

The scriptures testify that gifts and callings come without repentance. This statement is so powerful. We quote it so much until we at times we become blind to the fact that it reveals that no matter what spiritual state we are in, God will never revoke the gift/s that he has given us since the beginning of time. It does not matter if we are striving to enter into holiness or if we are deliberately sinning, we can rest assured that our gifts will work for us and at times to the benefit of others. Familiarity can be defined as the quality of being well known; recognizability based on long or close association. (Dictionary from Oxford) This spirit operates by stealth. It is undetected until someone that is walking in the spirit can identify it and its origin. Familiarity can gain information by lingering in atmospheres filled with words of prophecy and information. It can discern when a vessel needs uplifting and then it makes its move by saying all of the right and accurate things. You see, when a person is upset or down in their spirit, rarely do they remember the good things that God had previously said. This is a perfect time for this spirit to come and make its appearance. It camouflages itself behind words of truth, yet the motives are impure.

How can I identify this false gift from that of a true gift of prophecy?

This demonic influence can only be discerned through the spirit. It looks like and operates much like that of the true prophet until it almost seems impossible to detect. The Apostle Paul teaches us on how we must walk in the spirit. This is a key that he shares with the believer to keep them advantaged and aware of what is going on in the spirit world. When we decide to walk in this instruction, we give ourselves the opportunity to have the upper hand over the enemy in Jesus name.

How do I keep my spirit free from this spirit?

In the gospels, it teaches how that unclean spirits look for swept out and unoccupied vessels to dwell in. This means that in order to keep this spirit and any other unclean spirit from attaching itself to you or from possessing you, you must keep yourself full of God. Ask God to possess every fiber and every inch of your being.

What are examples of a familiar spirit?

A medium or spiritist. The terms medium and spiritist can be used interchangeably. Saul, the king, had banned all of the mediums and spiritists out of the land. This was probably because they were representations of bad omens and perhaps Saul did not want anything in his land that could bring a bad reproach. Read 1 Samuel 28:3

Why do we seek them?

1 Samuel 28:5-6. We can see how that fear of the known led to Saul's desperation to find a solution. Saul saw the philistine army and trembled greatly. However, we must note how Saul's first response was to consult the Lord, the urim process, a vision and dream from the Lord and then consultation with the prophets. It was when the Lord and the prophets and the other methods that he tried to get an answer from did not come through that he became desperate and arranged to see a medium. However, I believe that it was rejection that Saul felt that may have also caused Saul to take measures into his own hands through an act of desperation. Young prophet this is another reason why we must learn to reject the spirit of rejection that comes to provoke us to seek after validation

through ungodly means. It's ok with feeling rejected because everyone goes through it. Please do not allow this spirit to take residence in your life as it will only lead to harm. You will learn to quickly release these rejections that are sure to come in your life. We can also see through Scripture found in 1 Samuel 28:15 that another reason why we turn to familiar spirits is because many are deeply distressed. Saul said these words to the medium at En Dor, " I am deeply distressed." so let us recap on the three spirits that we have seen which can lead us to seek after familiar spirits and mediums for answers to make us feel secure:

▪ Rejection- refuse to grant or consider; feeling of dejection

▪ Desperation- hopelessness; despair

▪ Distressed- suffering from anxiety, sorrow, or pain

What do familiar spirits do?

According to 1 Samuel 28:8, familiar spirits operate in necromancy. They are communicators of the dead according to 1 Samuel 28:13-14. They perform seances to bring up the dead in order that they may communicate with them to gain information that is hidden. Let's look at 1 Samuel 28:11.

Why should we not entertain familiar spirits?

According to 1 Samuel 28:15-19. we see how that Saul is now operating as that of a medium and spiritist. Saul is now communicating with a familiar spirit whereas before he never had done such an evil act. Some people say that there is nothing wrong with communicating with the dead. However, as a prophet that is to be a pure and holy vessel unto the Lord, you cannot afford to open yourself up to these demonic spirits because you will become tainted. When you are tainted you will clog up your spirit from being able to receive the spiritual things from the Lord. In 1 Samuel 28 - we see how that Saul had the spirit of Samuel conjured up because he felt as though Samuel was more powerful than God and could possibly change the fate of his doomed future. This is another reason as to why we should never seek after familiar spirits is because we will start to hold them in higher regard than the Lord. This is dangerous.

Part 9: Faith and Prophecy

In this section we will see how that faith, love and prophecy work hand in hand. 1 Corinthians 13:2, "If I have the gift of prophecy and can fathom all mysteries and all knowledge, and if I have a faith that can move mountains, but do not have love, I am nothing." Faith is a commodity while operating in the office of a prophet. Faith activates the prophets motor. Without this faith you will see how that the prophet will not be empowered to move forward in order that he might operate from the highest place of his calling. He will become stifled. His prophetic ministry will become stale and though he will try to tap into a fresh place in the prophetic, he will be denied access. Faith is his key to move forward along with God's permission. In this section, you will see how having faith can help develop the prophet's boldness and level of confidence while moving in prophecy. You will see how that faith will cause the prophet to soar into places in the spirit with God causing his eyes and ears to see and hear things that are mysterious. With faith the prophet of God will not be afraid to walk through realms of the spirit with God and to open his mouth to say things that have yet to be known by man. Faith, the faith of God is needed in this ministry.

Hebrews 11:6, teaches us that without faith it is impossible to please the Lord. Walking as a prophet in the office of the prophetic we must possess faith. Faith is the foundation of all things possible. The prophetic realm calls for the prophetic vessel to operate fully in faith. The prophet will undergo a series and a lifetime of hearing uncommon instructions from the Lord. It will be imperative for him to be fully in faith. Let's examine what faith looked like in the life of a prophet.

Having faith is a commodity for the prophet as well as any believer that would allow space for it to operate in their daily lives. It is my understanding that God has dealt unto every man a measure of faith. It is my belief that faith is the foundation of all things possible. If we can get a hold of faith, we can get anything that God has ordained for us to possess. "Without faith it is impossible to please God..." (Hebrews 11:6) For the prophet, having faith is a partnership with God. It unlocks many doors for the prophet of God to gain access. If the people believe that anyone who cometh to God must believe that he rewards them that seek him, then the prophet must approach God with an open heart and a readiness to receive what he is approaching God for. The prophet's faith proves to God that he believes that he can perform the thing that he is petitioning him for.

The prophetic walk is a walk of faith. Remember that a prophesier can only prophesy what was revealed to him by way of the spirit. However, the one who walks in the office of a prophet can prophesy at will. This means that the prophet will step out on faith to declare that God will provide something (healing, new home, new job, new building etc), before other people and will have to depend on his faith to see God manifest it.

It is the prophet's faith that will help him to move forward with believing God for things that seem impossible to have. This is just it, for the prophet he finds great joy in challenges. This allows space for him to work his faith and to see God's hand moving in any situation. His greatest pleasure is seeing how God can make things happen for those with whom they have faith for. "Now" faith helps the prophet's ministry to:

▢ Take risks (Hebrews 11:8)

▢ receive supernatural strength to conceive and bear promise though you are overdue/past age bracket (Hebrews 11:11)

▢ Speak what's not into existence despite current circumstances (Hebrews 11:3)

▢ Tenacity to sow seeds in excellence (Hebrews 11:4)

▢ Sacrifice what's dear to you with belief that God can replenish you with greater (Hebrews 11:17-19)

▢ Bless others even when your season is almost over (Hebrews 11:21)

▢ prepare others for things to come (Hebrew 11:20)

Faith is the key to prophetic succession. Yes, the progression of your ministry will not be done without faith. As your faith grows, so will your reach. The higher you elevate in faith will reflect the level of boldness that you have to reach higher. Faith provokes confidence and boldness. It will be your faith which causes you to withstand long periods of endurance. You won't mind waiting because you have vision from God which speaks of a rewarding end if you wait. (Hebrews 11:35-36)

Part 10: Get Your Fruit Ripe

What is the fruit of the spirit? Why is it important to have this fruit? In this section we will explore why we as prophets should strive to walk in the fruit of the spirit of the Lord. You will see how it distinguishes you from that of a false prophet.

According to Galatians 5:22, the fruit of the spirit is not a wide variety of different fruit that can be separated. I would like to liken the fruit of the spirit to a piece of candy called Everlasting Gobstopper. Like this Everlasting Gobstopper, it is one fruit with many different layers of flavor. According to the Apostle Paul, the fruit of the spirit encompasses: love, joy, peace, kindness, faith, patience, long-suffering, gentleness and being sober-minded. This fruit of the spirit cannot be exemplified through the life of a person unless they have the Holy Spirit. The fruit of the spirit is one characteristic with many manifestations which points to the evidence that the believer has the Holy Spirit. Without this fruit the prophet will fulfill 1 John 2:16 which is to walk in the lust of the flesh, the lust of the eyes, and the pride of life which cometh not from the father but from the world.

For the prophet, partnership with the Holy Spirit is vital. John 13:35 reveals the words of Jesus to his disciples in that their love for one another would prove to the world that they were his disciples. This scripture points to the fact that our walk in the spirit is not only about us but about being a light in the world that they might see the unity that Christ represents. It is impossible for you to produce the fruit of the Spirit without the spirit. This is why your choice to walk in the spirit is connected to how well you are able to produce.

What are the works of the flesh? Exactly how do they affect my ministry? Why should I abandon them?

According to Galatians 5:18-20, the works of the are: adultery(sex with someone that's not your spouse); fornication(sex outside of marriage); uncleanness; lewdness; idolatry (worship towards anything besides God); sorcery (witchcraft); hatred (mean-spirited; lack of love); contentions; jealousies; outbursts; selfish ambition ; dissensions; heresies (unbelief); envy ; murders; drunkenness and revelries. These can also be synonymous with what it will look like in perilous times found in 2 Timothy 3:1-5. All of such which we are admonished to turn away from.

Making the choice to walk in the flesh will negatively influence your life. You will choose the way of men instead of the way of the Lord. The flesh loves to be praised. The reason why it is at enmity with God is because it seeks the place of God. Yes, the flesh seeks to stay alive so that it may rise to the seat of your life where only God should be exalted. The truth is that whatever we exalt reveals what we hold most valuable. Whatever is valuable in our lives becomes the dominant influencer in our lives. For the

Prophet this is dangerous if he or she chooses to walk under the auspices of their flesh. It would become the constant cause as to why their fruit is bitter and never sweet.

What is the fruit of the spirit? Why should I choose to walk therein?

According to Galatians 5:21-22, the fruit of the spirit are love; joy; peace; kindness; faith; patience; long-suffering; gentleness and being sober-minded. Choosing to walk out the fruit of the spirit will cause you to inherit the kingdom of God. This means that wherever you go you will exemplify what the kingdom of God looks like among men. In doing so, shall many be drawn and won over by the light of Christ Jesus and into salvation.

What causes me to become tied and entangled with the works of the flesh?

Walking in the lust of the flesh opens up a door for you to entertain the works of the flesh. According to Galatians 6:8(a) if we sow to the flesh, we will reap corruption. You may be wondering how you can have access to walk in the fruit of the spirit? Galatians 5:16; 5:24 teaches us that we must become Christs. Galatians 5:25 teaches that we can gain this access by choosing to live in the spirit.

Am I condemned because of my temptation of fleshly desires?

The bible teaches us that there is no condemnation to those who are in Christ Jesus and who walk not after the flesh. You are not condemned if you are being tempted by the devil. It is his job to tempt you with sowing into your flesh. This is where he can trap you in order to use you for his filthy gain. His plans are to lure you into entanglement that could take you years before you are totally delivered and free. Galatians 5:21- says that those who practice such will not inherit the kingdom of God. If you are acting on these ungodly temptations you are condemned as long as you are non- repentant. However, if you are not committing the sin that the devil is tempting you with, then you are still in Christ and are not condemned.

How does Satan draw me in?

1. Through persuasion (Galatians 5:8); (Genesis 3)

2. He tries to convince you that enjoying a little sin is ok. In actuality it could lead to decades of bondage. 20 minutes of "flesh gratification" can lead to 25 years of you wrestling for your freedom again. (Galatians 5:9)

Am I able to stand against the devil's temptation?

Yes, with the assistance of the Holy Spirit. (Galatians 5:16; Jude 24)

If I fall prey to the devil's tactics can I be redeemed? Absolutely! Romans 8:1-2; 2 Corinthians 5:17

How can I stay free?

Inquire of the Holy Spirit to help you to live out Jude 24. Believe that God can keep you from falling into the traps that the devil sets up to bring a reproach against God and my ministry. Believe that He will suffer a way for your escape. Speak what you believe. I believed therefore I speak. Open your mouth and speak the standard of God to be evident in your life young prophet.

Part 11: Lying Prophet or False Prophet

Lying prophet or false prophet? Let's talk about it. In this section you will see how you can be a prophet of God and lie. You will also see how you cannot be false and be a true prophet of God.

I know you may be wondering what the difference is between a lying prophet and a false prophet. You might be thinking if a liar should be deemed as false. I'm glad you are thinking along these lines because I had the same thoughts when I heard this in my spirit. I even questioned and inquired of the Lord on if my speculations centered around such thoughts were from a pure spirit. After about 3 months of asking God for clarity, I believe that I have finally been assisted by the Holy Spirit. Deuteronomy 18:22, (HCSB) "When a prophet speaks in the LORD's name, and the message does not come true or is not fulfilled, that is a message the LORD has not spoken. The prophet has spoken it presumptuously. Do not be afraid of him." According to Merriam's Dictionary, this word presumptuously means that one is overstepping due bounds (as of propriety or courtesy) : taking liberties. What this means is that one can be a true prophet of the Lord but that he or she is operating under a spirit of error. This also means that they are out of order and are operating from their own right and not from under the Lords jurisdiction. This is dangerous because as seen in the Scripture found in Deuteronomy 18:22, the prophet can influence the minds of God's people causing them to believe and trust in a lie. This is borderline witch craft. Notice how in this scripture that the prophet is not called false, but that he is deemed to be a liar because his words did not speak truth. So, we can see that it is possible to be a prophet of God but visited by a lying spirit. Let's examine 2 prophets in the bible that were indeed prophets but battled with a lying spirit:

- Abraham- Genesis 12:11;13;18-19- Abram, the prophet, lacked integrity as he lied and had Sarai to lie to save his life.

- Old prophet- 1 kings 13:1;18- an old senior prophet lied to a young and immature prophet.

Lying prophets are prophets that love God but who speak in error. Let's examine some traits of lying prophets:

- Called by God to be a prophet

- Love God

- Stand for what God represents

- Have a heart for God and people

- Compassionate

- May speak erroneous doctrine but can stand to be corrected

- Walk in the fruit of the spirit

What does it mean to be a false prophet? Do they even exist? Let's look at what the scripture says about false prophets:

- Matthew 7:15 ESV - "Beware of false prophets, who come to you in sheep's clothing but inwardly are ravenous wolves."

- 1 John 4:1 ESV -"Beloved, do not believe every spirit, but test the spirits to see whether they are from God, for many false prophets have gone out into the world."

- Matthew 24:24 ESV - "For false christs and false prophets will arise and perform great signs and wonders, so as to lead astray, if possible, even the elect."

- 2 Peter 2:1 ESV - "But false prophets also arose among the people, just as there will be false teachers among you, who will secretly bring in destructive heresies, even denying the Master who bought them, bringing upon themselves swift destruction."

To be false simply means that something or someone was never "it" from the beginning. According to Merriam Dictionary, to be false means not genuine, authentic, or legitimate. It means that something or someone is not according to truth or fact. When someone is a lying prophet it means that they are prophets but their words are wrong. However, to be a false prophet goes beyond words and now is about how their whole being or declaration as being a prophet is false. The bible points out signs of what a false represents or look like. Let's examine some of these traits:

- Never ordained a prophet by God

- Never sent by God

- Inwardly ravenous wolves

- Possess not the fruit of the spirit

- Hath not a love for the true and living God

- Speak contrary of God's word

- Quote the bible but under a false spirit

- Cannot stand to be corrected because truth irritates them

We as prophets are always listening out for revelation from the Lord. Prophets like to hear from God because it brings out a holy and righteous confidence in them. However, even with our correct hearing we as prophets can have a wrong interpretation about the thing/s that we have correctly seen. Let's look at a lesson that God puts the young prophet Jeremiah through found in Jeremiah 1:11-15,

"Moreover, the word of the Lord came unto me, saying, Jeremiah, what seest thou? And I said, I see a rod of an almond tree. Then said the Lord unto me, thou hast well seen: for I will hasten my word to perform it. And the word of the Lord came unto me the second time, saying, what seest thou? And I said, I see a seething pot; and the face thereof is toward the north. Then the Lord said unto me, out of the north an evil shall break forth upon all the inhabitants of the land. For, lo, I will call all the families of the kingdoms of the north, saith the Lord; and they shall come, and they shall set everyone his throne at the entering of the gates of Jerusalem, and against all the walls thereof roundabout, and against all the cities of Judah. And I will utter my Judgments against them touching all their wickedness, who have forsaken me, and have burned incense unto other gods, and worshipped the works of their own hands."

We see how God puts the prophet Jeremiah through a test by allowing his vision to elevate and then asking him what he saw. Notice how that the prophet Jeremiah did not go over and abroad on what God allowed for him to see. Jeremiah did not try to impress God with lofty words. He simply gave God back what was truly revealed to him. This honesty was the key needed for Jeremiah to have access into true and in depth meaning of the word of the Lord. God then began to help Jeremiah's understanding and interpretation on what was revealed to him. Oftentimes when we hear from God or when we have been allowed to see into the mind of God, we want to immediately share it. When we do not have the full meaning of the thing that God has revealed then what will happen is that the prophet will operate from under a spirit of presumption. They will begin to "speak" presumptuously. The word that they give or the interpretation that is given will be delivered as a "true" prophetic word from the Lord when indeed it is not. This is called a lying prophet. You may ask, "Well if what they said is not a true word, does not this make them false?" I say to you absolutely not. There have been patriarchal and matriarchal prophets and even prophets today that have truly been called and chosen to walk as prophets in the earth that have given wrong interpretations on the true vision or dream from the Lord. They saw correctly but just because their interpretation of that word was off does not make them a false prophet, however, it does mean that they lied and therefore can be called a liar in that moment. But, wait a minute do not give up hope as I have said many prophets have gone through this stage of prophetic development. What it does is that it helps the prophet to become more cautious when releasing words supposedly "from the Lord." It provokes them to pray and seek the face of God and wise counsel before presenting the "revelation" with anyone. I heard one Prophet say that, "If you never mess up, then that means you are God. If you do mess up that means that you are human."

I feel led to testify at this moment. During the presidential election between Hillary Clinton and Donald Trump there was great anticipation. There was confusion because there were some prophets that said that God showed them that Hillary would win and then there were other prophets that said that Donald Trump would win. I have never been interested in politics. However, I had 2 dreams about the election. In the first dream I saw Hillary Clinton rise to victory but how that would be a struggle due to some deception with the poll counts. I went about my way and approximately two weeks later I was at my parent's house and had come into the house to take a nap. When I sat on the couch I fell into a sleep. As soon as my eyes shut, I went into another dream. In this dream I was in a little room with Hillary Clinton again and I was so excited. In the center of the room was a plain round wooden table. I looked at Hillary and said, "Well, Hillary how do you feel now that you will win the presidential election?" When Hillary looked at me, I was thrown away because her facial expression was disheartening. Hillary then banged her fits on the wooden round table with fury and yelled, "Ugh! I cannot believe this. I just did not see this coming. I never saw it coming!" I had come out of the dream with confusion. I dwelled on the two dreams for about a couple of days but never really prayed into what was revealed. I then took what was revealed both times and said to myself, "Oh, this must mean that Hillary will win but she will have to undergo some great curve balls, but she'll win, oh she's got to win." Oh, I went and shared with people that God had revealed to me who would win. To make a long story short when the Election Day had come and Donald Trump won, I was shocked. "NO!!!!" I thought. God but you showed me Hillary winning.

God helped my understanding in that things had shifted, and he did reveal it to me but how I did not press into prayer to grab the true meaning of both dreams. Dream #1 revealed how that Hillary would indeed win but how that there would be some deception before the conclusion of the matter. Indeed, there was some deception that came out with poll numbers and everything. However, in dream # 2, God was showing me how there would be a shift due to something happening that would cause an upset with Hillary and this whole election. When Hillary kept saying how she never thought it would go the way it did, that was God showing me that though she thought that she had the election and would win, it would not end up that way and thus cause her to be thrown for a loop.

I encourage all prophets to really pray about what you see. It is possible to see correctly but because of poor seeking, come out with a wrong interpretation. I had become lazy in my approach because the things that I would dream of in my sleep leading up to those election dreams had come true. This caused me to not feel the need to really press in with praying to God about what I had seen concerning Hillary Clinton. This taught me a great lesson that I should never become lazy in my approach to interpreting dreams. So, I leave you with this young prophet, SEEK GOD ABOUT ALL THAT YOU SEE.

Part 12: The Prophet and Sexual Perversion

Are you a prophet but secretly dealing with a spirit of sexual perversion? Have you ever asked yourself why so many prophets wrestle with a sexually perverted spirit? In this section we will discuss why this is a major attack against the mouthpieces of the Lord. We will discuss why it's important to keep your vessels clean of all sexual sins.

There are churches in operation today with men who are married to other men known as first gentlemen and women who are married to women. This is an abomination in the sight of the Lord and he disapproves of this type of behavior. God loves the fornicator, adulterer and homosexual, but he does not agree with their acts. God can deliver.

Before we began this lesson, I would like to go over some terminology that you might see repeatedly used. let us define these words:

▪ Perversion - diverting from the true intent or purpose; a change to something worse; a turning or applying to a wrong end or use. (Webster) It is a satanic twist of anything that God has performed.

▪ Homosexuality- sexual orientation toward members of one's own gender

▪ Bi-sexuality- strong confusion over whether one should have sexual orientation towards members of the opposite sex or sexual attraction over members of one's own gender

⧠ Hetero-sexual- sexual orientation towards members of the opposite gender

⧠ Abomination - extreme disgust and hatred. (Webster)

⧠ Desolation- devastation, ruin, grief, sadness. (Webster)

Once again according to the word, it teaches us that gifts and callings come without repentance. Indeed, when Christ was ascending up towards heaven, he also did choose men to descend gifts upon. This choosing of who should have whatever gift given was a direct partnership between the ascending Christ and the descending Holy Spirit. When you were chosen to receive your prophetic mantle, you were chosen because God felt as if you were the right one for a specific prophetic purpose under heaven. When gifts were descended, they were done so in its purest form. Young prophet I want you to realize that when you see perverted prophets, know that they did not start out this way. Somewhere along their journey they were introduced to sexual perversion through another person, pornography, social media (television, radio,etc.), molestation, rape or a sexually demonic spirit. However, ultimately the driving force behind sexual perversion is demonic persuasion.

Some of you may be wondering how a sexually perverted prophet can still operate in this gift of prophecy. I'm glad you asked. The vessel is unclean, and the gift is unclean. This must mean that the prophecies are unclean too. Though what is said can be accurate, the spirit in which it is released is tainted and impure. Let us look at how this prophetic gift function under two different spirits starting with how the prophet operates while in the purity of the gift:

Spirit of God

The motives are pure. The prophetic vessel has access into the deep things of the spirit. The prophetic vessel is able to discern the deep mysteries of God. This pure prophetic vessel has been given true access to discern the prophetic future and solutions of the Lord. Its prophecies are not stale and old. He springs forth into the newness of the Lord. Because he is pure, he brings forth new wine. His prophetic wells are filled with fresh waters sufficient enough to quench the thirst of those that drink from it. His table is filled with fresh prophetic dainties fit to satisfy the hunger that roars within. This pure prophet can operate at such a level because he moves in the purity of the Lord. His ears are fine-tuned that he might hear as well as to discern the meaning of what the Spirit of the Lord is saying to the church. he moves with the frequency of the spirit and therefore can move confidently with the movements of prophecy. If the Lord changes his mind about something that he heard him say in the last season, this prophet does not become frantic. He remains sure in his calling. He is sure that God will speak to him again. He knows that God will validate him with whatever comes forth out of his prophetic spirit.

Let's examine how this gift works to deceive many:

Spirit of darkness

The motives are impure. Deception and manipulation are it's driving force. It appears to have access to the deep things of the spirit, but it doesn't. It rides off what was last prophesied and couples it with what is evident in the natural realm and presents it as the secrets of the Lord. It is not a servant of God ye it has not the true secret of the Lord. Therefore, the spirit of the Lord says unto us (the church), he that hath an ear let him hear what the spirit of the Lord is saying unto the church. The perverted vessel is not given permission to move into the hidden prophetic of the Lord, yet it seeks to appear as if it has been given access.

Gift without repentance

This means that though the gift is still yours who is the governing force over it? Just because God will not take your gift back does not mean that he is obligated to sanction you while you are in your perversion. In the moments of your perversion you are gifted by God but governed by the devil. Ephesians 2:20 says that "God built the foundation of his church upon His HOLY apostles and His HOLY prophets with Christ Jesus himself as the Chief Cornerstone." The devil fights prophets with sexual perversion (especially same sex) attraction because he need prophetic vessels to lay false foundation that the church maybe built upon it. If the devil can get the apostles and prophets, whom that Lord originally wanted to use to lay his true foundation upon the church, to promote what

66

caters to peoples flesh and ideologies as truth, we are in trouble. The church would be highly gifted but doctrinally backwards. This is the agenda of the devil in that he does not mind you being gifted as a prophet just as long as your message promotes a blinding message. The attack is not merely on the prophet or the church as much as it is against God and what he stands for, which is holiness and right living. The devil wants us shouting while going down a path that leads to death and destruction. Young prophet, you may be tempted but you are surely not tainted. If you do not commit the act, then you are ok. However, ask God to keep you from the very desire to operate in wrong sexual activity. God is able to keep you from failing even when your flesh is not willing.

Part 13: Major Spiritual Attacks

The spirit of pride is a major attack against prophets. This spirit fights to enter in and use the prophet in order that the prophet would miss their destiny in God. God hates pride. Many prophets in the beginning stages of their growth and development do not receive rebuke well. They fail to believe that while a holy rebuke may not feel good to their flesh, it comes to turn them toward the more righteous path. Rebuke is redirection wrapped in affliction. They will begin to think that because they can hear God that no one should tell them what to do but God. We will discuss how this is connected to the same incident with Miriam and Aaron and why we should never entertain a spirit as such. Let's examine the main spirits that attack the prophets of God:

Lying spirit-

1. 1 kings 13:1;18- an old senior prophet lies to a young and immature prophet.

2. 1 Samuel 15:13-15;19-21;24 -Saul was not a prophet but a prophesier and lied.

3. Genesis 12:11;13;18-19- Abram, the prophet, lacks integrity as he lied and had Sarai to lie to save his life.

4. Jeremiah 23:1-32- These prophets were lying prophets

Fear - 1 Kings 19:2-3 -prophet Elijah is overcome with fear by a false prophetic voice by the name of Jezebel. As a prophet, there are three things that you do not do when battling a spirit of fear:

1. never go alone- 1 kings 19:3

2. never settle in a wilderness place- 1 Kings 19:4- This represents places where there is no water or bread to sustain you through this season of your life... do not go into dry houses where the word of the Lord is not found. Do not seek mentors or leadership who are dry and non-efficient

3. never keep travelling- 1 kings 19:4- while battling with this spirit of fear which caused torment, he still kept going. There are sometimes when the prophet should stop and take a reprieve to receive help from the Lord

God will not leave us fearful. Let's look at some of the scriptures found in the book of the prophets which reveals that God will not leave the prophet to be bound by this spirit of fear:

1. Jeremiah 1:8 (NIV)- "Do not be afraid of them, for I am with you and will rescue you," declares the LORD."

2. Ezekiel 2:6- (NLT) "Son of man, do not fear them or their words.."

Doubt - In Jeremiah 1:6-7- the prophet Jeremiah doubts that he could do this prophetic assignment due to 2 things:

> 1. he feels as if his speech is not mature enough- in the prophetic it's not merely about the eloquence of your speech as much as it is that you have a word and the ability to syntactically put them together so that the true meaning of it is revealed

> 2. he was a youth- Jeremiah felt as if him being young disqualified him from being able to carry a prophetic word until full term

Another good example of this is looking through the story of Gideon. Though Gideon was not a prophet, he was a man of valor and a man whom the Lord had chosen in a very prophetic season. He was chosen by God to do a work but doubted. Examine his story in Judges 6:12-15 and see that even though he was dealing with this doubt how that the Lord did not leave him to waddle in this doubt.

Inferior Complex- Exodus 3:10-11; 4:10 expresses the inferior complex of a man who was deemed to be the humblest man on earth. However, when approached and chosen by the Lord to become the deliverer of Israel; he felt inferior to his assignment. Moses felt inferior because of his speech issue and possibly because he probably had never done an assignment as big as that before. Though Moses had been in the house of a pharaoh as a heathen, the Lord was sending him back as a redeemed man with a different message and under a different mandate. This time he was to deliver.

70

Identity dysfunction (not normal) - This spirit comes to prey on the persona of the prophet to make them abandon who they are while striving to become someone else. This is the spirit that causes many people to embrace a false identity. I will say this young prophet, being a youth with a major prophetic assignment can become weighty. This is the reason why so many ask God to take away their prophetic activation or ability. They want to be like the other youth and be lenient and to have good leisure. The fact is that God will grant the space for some to not fully operate in their calling until older but then there are some of you where the Lord will burden with a prophetic call to service early on. If this is you, please do not abandon who you are just to fit in with the other youth who are not prophetic. God wants to raise you up to be a resource of strength and a voice of reason for your generation. God will never leave a generation without a prophetic voice to provide direction. YOU ARE IT. Don't miss your opportunity to be raised up as a young prophetic leader in this hour.

Arrogance/pride - Most prophets battle with spirits of pride and arrogance. Not all, but some prophets have problems with following leadership or authoritative figures mostly because they are in some type of authority position themselves. However, another reason why prophets have a hard time with following leadership is due to past abuse from leadership. Typically, with these prophets, it is not until God heals them on the inside that they will hold up walls and dare anyone to tamper with them. These walls are some of the reasons why some prophets do not ascend into their next prophetic dimension with God.

Another reason why prophets become arrogant and prideful is because they have seen messy leadership and have decided not to allow anyone to tell them what to do. This is dangerous because God could have sent them their help but they will see them as hurt instead and thus miss out on receiving an inheritance if not healed. Other reasons as to why the prophet operates under a demonic spirit of arrogance and pride is as follows:

1. they feel as if they have arrived

2. self-entitlement

3. lack of training

4. lack of gift development

5. dissatisfaction

Satan (Isaiah) and King Nebuchadnezzar are good examples of this arrogance and pride. Miriam and Aaron

Depression is another enemy of the prophetic walk. Often because of the weight of the assignment and the burdens that comes with it, it can bring on depression. The prophet must forever decide to make the presence of the Lord their home. In this section we will discuss how important it is for the prophet to help people get through life but to never carry their lives.

Part 14: The Voice of the Prophet

You are a voice. John the Baptist, who was a prophet of the Lord declared these words, "I am a voice crying out in the wilderness prepare ye the way of the Lord." In this section we will discuss 3 things: self- discovery, scope of your calling, the message in your voice and more.

Self-discovery

Though you are a voice, you are not chosen to be a voice for every matter under the heavens. Your voice will be heard the loudest when you have learned and accepted the prophetic sphere to which you were anointed to oversee in the spirit. This can only happen through self- discovery. The question that should be asked is how does one evade into true self-discovery? This is a packed question because it's going into the identity of the personal side of who this prophet is. We will deal with this a little bit more in another section.

Scope of your Calling

The scope of your calling can only be identified by God. He is the one that called you to such ministry. I want you to know that if you are called to sit with presidents and politicians like the prophet Daniel, or called to go into the low places to deliver God's people like the prophet Moses know that you are valuable. Your voice matters. Never look at the high or low numbers of support from man. They can be fickle. Instead be like the prophet David and look to the hills from which cometh your help. It will come from people at times but your number one supporter will be God. Go forth prophet.

The Message in your Voice

Young prophet you have got to know that you are a voice. God has chosen you to be a prophet (acting as God in the earth) by functioning as his voice into the spiritual hearing of those that are spiritual. You must realize that you have a message in your belly which has the potency to penetrate the lives of those who would give ear. The scriptures says, "He that hath an ear, let him hear what the spirit is saying to the church." Jesus said these words because he wanted people to know that if they were going to benefit from his message, they had to be walking in the spirit. Young prophet your words are spiritual. Yes, in your voice lies spirit and life. Jesus spoke and said that the words that I speak are both spirit and life. What this means is that you are carrying a powerful weapon in your voice which are spirit (liberty; freedom) and life (living). Your prophetic voice has been given by God for the church to bring forth edification and perfection through the words that spring forth from your lips.

John the Baptist is a prime example of how relevant and authoritative your voice can be as a prophet of God. John 1:23 reveals how that when asked who you are you don't use it as an opportunity to exalt yourself or your accomplishments. This John reveals how true prophetic voices always use rare moments as these as a means to exalt Christ. God has always given prophetic voices as a means to prepare to meet Christ. Prophetic voices are so relevant in that they come forth as a bull dozier to perform these 6 authorities:

1. Root out

2. Pull down

3. Destroy

4. Overthrow

5. Build

6. Plant

Notice in Jeremiah 1:10 how that his prophetic voice was given him by the Lord and thus had already given him vocal elevation to become a resounding sound. However, this prophetically authoritative voice has not been given as a means for abuse. You need to know that your voice will be most effective in the region or under the prophetic rank given you. Notice in Jeremiah 1:7 how God told Jeremiah that he should go to all whom he sent him to and to use his voice as directed by God. This proves to us prophets that we do not pick and choose with whom our voices are amplified for. God chooses the places where he wants our voices to be heard. If we would be given this luxury of choosing, we would only choose our family, friends and the people we like. We would hardly choose people who are hard to love, unpleasant to be around, those who are rebellious and those who are stiff-necked. These are the kinds of people that make our prophetic calling a little difficult to enjoy. That's just it; prophetic voices are normally chosen and sent to be the voice of reason, logic, love and compassion to those who are hard to care for and to be around. Some examples in the bible of prophets sent to hard places were as follows:

1. Jonah- chosen to go deliver Nineveh out of their sins

2. Ezekiel- called to be a prophetic voice to a rebellious people

3. Daniel- dealt with jealous and evil governors and satraps

4. Jeremiah- sent to be a voice to kings, priests, false prophets and people who did not value him as a person or a prophet.

5. Elijah- sent to deal with wicked kings and prophets

Juanita Bynum turned down the open invitation to preach at a church in Maryland. It is my belief that she testified of her doing this to help young prophets know that every door was not for you to walk in at the time of the open invitation. She said that at the times that the Pastor had invited her, God had not given her a word for that church house. This kind of behavior is only done through mature prophets who are not looking for fame or money on account of the use of their prophetic gifting or office. It was not until years later that the Lord had begun to deal with her concerning that church; as a result she went to preach. One day turned into almost a two-week revival. Young prophet, when you allow God to choose where and when you go, you will most likely find that there are multiple assignments for you to do while there. You are bigger than fame and a check. You carry prophetic revival in your spirit. No amount of money can conjure this up and out of your spirit.

As prophets we do not use our voices as a weapon to abuse the authority given us. We are given influence to speak forth truth. When you speak to someone life should be impacted. We are not to be bought. Never allow people to manipulate your message from God. be authentic and true to your calling. Carry out your message. Remember, though men may applaud you or not; your ultimate goal is to speak for God so that in the end you will be rewarded with hearing him say, "Well done thy good and faithful servant."

Part 15: Prophetic Seclusion

This section is absolutely NOT about prophets being lone rangers. Let me make this clear that though prophets are called to be consecrated or separated does not mean that they will not have people to interact with throughout the course of their lives. To think that prophets are called to do life alone is demonic allusion. God has called us to fellowship with people on the earth. To make it clear, no one will be able to fulfill their destinies without having some kind of holy communion with the people that God has called them to walk within the earth.

In this section you will find that when you are called to be a prophet of God your circle will typically be small. You will discover that many will be called to the prophetic side of you but few to the person. We will discuss how you must embrace this level of sacrifice.

To be secluded means to be separated; set-apart; to be isolated. As we look through both the old and new testament, we can see that many of the Lord's prophets were secluded for various reasons. Some seclusions were God ordained and used as a means of security and reprieve. Others were provoked by demonic intimidation to isolate the prophet away from his or her assignment as well as to take him or her away from atmospheres and people that could serve as divine strength to them.

Some prophets go into seclusion under the guise of being called by "God" there. They believe that this "God" calling them into seclusion will somehow cause them to be granted access into realms of power and prophetic insights." Many immature or young prophets are at times so very zealous for the things of God until they do not know that every pull to seclude themselves is not a call from the Lord. They at times fail to realize that not all separations are ordained by God.

Some prophets are more sentimental than others. What this means is that their tolerance levels for offenses, hurts, disrespect, etc.. are low and due to their soft hearts, they are easily influenced to quickly run to dark secluded places. They do not know that sometimes God allows for such pains to hit the prophet's lives in order to propel them into greater prophetic spherical places in Him. Running at the cause of man's immaturity and ignorance provides a means for them to hide from the things that's causing them emotional disturbances. This ungodly seclusion is a direct set up from the devil to lure them into his demonically false physic sphere. Sentimental prophets are those that approach their pastors to inform them that the "Lord" has impressed upon their hearts to go on a 90-day sabbatical. This however, is on account of the Lord having to reveal some great revelation with them. Oftentimes it's not the Lord but whether the devil that is luring them to a place away from humanity because they feel bruised, tattered, torn and in need of healing. In my opinion it's ok to be in a state of needing inner healing, we all do. As a matter of fact, it is because prophets are in more seasons of warfare than down-time and they need time off to be alone. However, the problem lies in the fact that instead of the prophet being truthful with, "why" they need to separate, they make it seem as though all is well when indeed it is not. This means that the prophet is now dishonest and irresponsible with his emotional inner being.

What being phony does is that it leaves the prophet open to being more receptive to pre-conceived ideas from the enemy. It is in times like these, when the devil will have a field day on the mind and emotions of the prophet. It is in seasons like these where the prophet would seem to believe a lie more so than the truth. This is only because the devil has access to your hurts, your ear, your mind and your emotions. This is dangerous because it will leave you vulnerable to carry a lie in your spirit in which you will operate from. This could be destructive to your prophetic ministry, your relationships and your well-being. I admonish you before you take your hurt on a "self-ordained" sabbatical, to allow a mature saint into your inner issues to help pray you through. Don't use: seclusion" as a means to dismiss your inner worries but rather conquer them through exposure. (Use Elijah cave experience)

Other seclusions are God ordained. Let's examine some scriptural examples of "God ordained seclusions":

i. Obadiah- hides 100 of the Lord's prophets (security/protection from a murderous authority figure)

ii. John Baptist- was led for about 30 years to seclude away with God in order that he might be prepared to go serve people

80

iii. David- flees from Saul to the Cave of Adullam

iv. Jeremiah- the Lord tells him he was to be set apart

v. Apostle Paul- instructs us to come out from among them and to be ye separated according to the Lord.

Young prophet let God seclude you but when he lets you out; do yourself a favor and come out. you need balance and you need to interact with mankind. God has chosen you to reach people with your voice. Come out of hiding prophet and fellowship.

Part 16: The Misunderstood Prophet

In this section we will discuss how prophets are often misunderstood. This will sometimes breed enemies. This will also at times cause the prophet frustration. If not careful the prophet will want to give up and run to a secluded place.

Prophets are different. They live under the heavens' radar. They move to the beat of a different drum; therefore, their sound is unique. They smile when the world is frowning. They exemplify hope when others are in despair. They are drawn to the quiet places when the world is attracted to noise. They are normally the opposite of what others represent. They are the standard of God on the earth. This means that they are against what the world stands for.

When the prophet of God moves, he is moving based upon the instructions that are hidden from the average man. Others may look at the prophet as being a "defiant" person or "strange," but they must know that the prophet has a piece of information they do not have and is moving based upon revealed revelation. This at times causes friction between the prophet and those who are not prophetic. This friction only happens because people cannot understand why the prophet functions the way that they do. Oftentimes jealousy sets in the hearts of people who are not prophetic. This jealousy is due to the fact that they do not understand the "weird" behavior of the prophet. What seems strange to others is often the thing which produces miracles, signs and wonders for the prophet. A miracle from God almost never happens by way of common sense. The prophet is normally ready to look foolish before men in order to see the supernatural wonders of God revealed in the earth.

Let's examine some of the prophets who were misunderstood:

1. Jeremiah- The prophet Jeremiah had a ministry that was validated by the Lord. Though his ministry was blessed by God he paid a high price for it. He was constantly under fire, mocked, rejected and excluded by men for whom he was given the word of the Lord to give. This was because he did not prophesy a favorable word to them that would itch their ears or satisfy their evil deeds. He was misunderstood only because he had a different report than the false prophets. (Jeremiah 20:7-8)

2. Ezekiel- I'm sure when Ezekiel ate and drank with such dramatics that he was misunderstood. However, these dramatized prophetic acts had hidden messages in them for both Israel and Jerusalem, which were God's people. (Ezekiel 12:18-20)

3. Daniel- Daniel was misunderstood by the governors and satraps when he decided to keep his dedication by praying at his regular times though a decree had gone out for the citizens of the land to not pray for 30 days. Daniel was willing to risk his life for the cause of God. This is what true prophets do. However, in the end God vindicates them. (Daniel 6:4-9;11)

4. Hosea- I'm sure that those who looked on the prophet misunderstood his decision as a prophet by engaging with a woman of disgrace. However, the prophet was obeying the voice of the Lord as the marriage and the woman had great prophetic symbolism as it concerned God's chosen people Israel.

5. Elisha- The prophet Elisha was misunderstood. A man by the name of Naaman was a leper in need of healing. It was the prophet Elisha that gave the uncommon directive for Naaman to go and dip himself in the river Siloam, which was filthy waters. Naaman was already in a nasty situation and the prophet's instructions did not seem logical. However, it was when Naaman put aside his disagreeable stand point and followed through with the instruction that he received the healing that he was in need of. Once again miracles do not happen by common sense. (Read 2 kings 5:10-14)

Young prophet, please do not go and curl up in a corner all because you feel misunderstood by man. Yes, at times it can make you desire to keep silent in order to not have to explain the, "why's" to what you do. You must know that you are moving to the beat of a different drum. the conductor of your life is different, therefore how you move about life will be out of the box. It's ok. God will put you in the company of people like yourself and they will embrace you and your movements because they will understand you. #Keepmoving

Part 17: Persecution

Persecution is inevitable in the entire 5-fold ministry. However, there is no other ministry that I have seen more bashed than that of the ministry of the prophet. In this section we will look at what Jesus said about persecution. We will also look at how that persecution is never about the man but all about the messiah.

Being in any of the five-fold ministries or operating in any of the 9 gifts of the spirit can be rewarding. However, it can also become emotionally and mentally draining due to the persecution that is associated with having the privilege to walk in any gifting. It is my strongest belief that of all the ministry callings and gifts, it is the prophetic vessels that are the ones that undergo the greatest persecution with regard to the ministry of the Apostle. To be persecuted means to be under heavy malign or to be highly scrutinized. It is my understanding that prophets are fought because they come in the name of "God" and as a messenger on God's behalf. Prophets must mature to the place of knowing that it is not them that is being attacked as much as it is the message that they carry. Within the message of any true prophet is the exaltation of Christ the messiah. So, in reality the ultimate goal of persecution of the prophet is to keep Christ, the messiah from being revealed through preaching. This means that any attack that the prophet undergoes should never be internalized or taken as offense on account of him but on account of Christ. (scripture on don't take offense the persecution is about Christ)

You may be wondering who these persecutions usually come through? Let's look at the prophet Jeremiah and who the Lord warned him in private about as it concerned persecution. Jeremiah 1:18:

☐ Kings

☐ Princes

☐ Priests

☐ People of the land

It's here in this private session with God that young Jeremiah is prepared to know who to expect persecution from. Young Jeremiah is taught from an early age that the persecution would be a direct target to his messages spoken to them. Look at verse "19": where the Lord says these words to the prophet, "for behold, I have made you this day 3 things:

1. Fortified city

2. Iron pillar

3. Bronze walls

See how the Lord reassures this young prophet that he is well equipped spiritually to handle the persecutions that were sure to come against him. Notice also how the Lord defines that this inner infrastructure strength would be given because the whole land of

Judah would attack him on account of his representation of God and because of his words. God had built Jeremiah and had given him prophetic authorities to work within the perimeters of "Judah." This shows us how that when God is preparing us, he does so in concordance with our prophetic assignment. In Jeremiah's case this was in Judah. Pause right now! Have you asked God for what people, nation and region of people he is preparing and giving you spiritual fortitude for? This will help you to not burden yourself with weights and assignments that are not your responsibility.

Let's look at the young prophet Ezekiel who was about 30 years old at the time the Lord called him into the prophetic ministry:

In Ezekiel 3:7, God assures the prophet on how the persecution against him would not really be about him but it would be against the God that he would speak for. Much like with the prophet Jeremiah, the Lord touched the prophet Ezekiel for the persecutions that were ahead of him in his prophetic journey. (Ezekiel 3:8-9)

Let's look at the young prophet Daniel who was about 17 years old at the time the Lord called him into the prophetic ministry:

Sometimes your prayer life can get you persecuted. The prophet Daniel went under great persecution from the governors and the satraps due to his dedication towards God. It seems as though most of the Lord's prophets are ridiculed on account of who they serve and are promoting, which is God in heaven and righteousness (Read: Daniel 6)

I can hear these words in my spirit, "Jerusalem! O Jerusalem! Why thou persecute the Lord's prophets? You have got to know that persecution is a part of the prophetic ministry. However, Matthew 10:25 says, "fear not for the intentions of the persecutions will be revealed." This means that the persecutions made against you will be known. Nothing done to you in the dark will remain in the dark. God will shine light on it and cause you to see with your eyes. you will win because you will know what devious plans are conjured against you. Pray! Relax! Stay focused! Keep producing!

Part 18: The Prophet and his Flaws

Embracing your flaws. In this section we will see how important it is for the young prophet to love themselves despite their "limitations."

Everyone has flaws. You need to know this young prophet. You need to know that the people that are always pointing out your flaws only do so because they are trying to conceal theirs. I want you to know that your flaws do not have enough influence to change God's mind about you. While people may reject you and abandon your prophetic gift, God will not discount you on behalf of hiccups that occur in your life. Every prophet that God used in the bible had flaws and yet God used them to do great exploits in their lifetime.

Having flaws can serve as a humbling tool for the prophet. When you know that God has called you to be on the frontline as his spokesman, it is often your ability to be in touch with your issues that keeps you in contact with God. God uses these flaws as a means to keep us seeking after him. Having flaws helps the prophet to access the power of God in their lives because of their humility. I remember attending a service with Marilyn Hickey. It was funny because a friend and I had just gotten out of another service and were invited to a quick birthday celebration. We were leaving the party so that we could make it in time to hear Marilyn Hickey. We discovered that we had a plate of food but no drink to wash it down, so we decided to get on the elevator to go back up to get something to drink. On our way up we bumped into Marilyn Hickey and her assistant. Wow! With food in our mouths and grease on our hands we politely said hello as we all laughed on that elevator. I told Marilyn Hickey that we were on our way to come hear her speak. She was elated. It was at that moment that I was embarrassed. There I was at the height of my flaw (over eating) that I felt so convicted. When we had gotten to church, we were seated in the front of the church. When Marilyn Hickey got up, she glanced over and saw us and she just paused. I got nervous because I thought that she was going to call us up there or something. However, the next words that came out of her mouth was this: "God is drawn to your frailties." Wow! There I was feeling guilty because I had just gotten through sinning by overeating. However, the Lord brought such comforting words to allow me to know that my overeating (flaw) would not shun him away from me but how that it would draw him closer to me. It was in that moment that I came to know that walking with God there is no embarrassment. God already sees and knows all.

I do not know who will get this book. Maybe you are battling like me with overeating. Maybe some of you are battling with high functioning depression, fornication, smoking weed, drinking, manipulation, thoughts of suicide etc... I want you to know that these things do not take God by surprise. God is not afraid of your battles. Man may not know how to deal with it because you are a functioning prophet and their hopes in you were high, but God knows what to do. He holds the key to your deliverance and your destiny.

I wanted to talk about this section because I have spoken privately to hundreds of people that were positioned in their churches as prophets, running revivals, etc.. but wrestling secretly with their flaws. While people were applauding them for how well they performed they were dying on the inside for lack of the necessary help that they needed to get better. Most times I would tell them that God cared for them and was not ignorant of the flaws that they were presently dealing with. I would encourage them to ask God to help them not desire whatever it was that was plaguing their soul. Some of them wanted to give in to the grips of their battles. They really felt harassed by them. Some admitted to confessing their faults but how it still did not go away. I suggested that they search their hearts to know if they really wanted to be free or if they were just saying so out of guilt. Jude 24.

Part 19: Signs of the Prophets

How you ever wondered if you were a prophet or not. Have you ever noticed that you were a little different than the neighbor across the street or your best friend? Do you ever have dreams and they always come to pass? Do you feel a higher calling to Holy living? Are you highly compassionate about praying for others in order to hear God on their behalf? Well these may be signs that you are a prophet of the Lord. In this section we will examine some of the signs that prophets identify with.

The most typical signs that you are a prophet are as follows:

- Your number 1 sign of knowing that you are a prophet is that God will create a unique way to reveal this to you:

  a. Numbers 12: 6-8

  b. Deuteronomy 34:10

- It is confirmed by others:

  - Prophets

    - 1 Samuel 9: 6

    - Mark 1 :2-4 (NASB 95)

  b. Angels

- Luke 1:17

c. Jesus

- Matthew 11: 9; 13

3. Drawn to pray/intercession:

a. Daniel 6:10

4. Drawn to holiness/lift up the standard of God:

a. Daniel 6:3-5

5. Drawn to nature/elements:

a. Exodus 3:2-4

6. Drawn to seclusion- Would rather spend the majority of their time with God than with man

7. Have a love and strong compassion for mankind- in particular the lowly and downtrodden

8. A worshipper in the high places of God:

a. 1 Samuel 10:5

b. Obadiah- means worshipper of Yaweh. Obadiah was a prophet of the Lord

9. Points man back to God:

    a. John the Baptist- Mark 1:4 (NLT)

10. Rejected: This happens as a preparation tool to help get the prophet ready for his/her prophetic ministry

    a. peers

    b. family members

    c. church members

    d. world

11. A strong desire to serve and please God than man

https://www.ashleyreynoldsministry.com/